FREDDIE & ME

D1373041

FREDDIE &ME

A Coming-of-Age (Bohemian) Rhapsody

MIKE DAWSON

BLOOMSBURY

COPYRIGHT © 2008 BY MIKE DAWSON

All rights reserved. No part of this book may be used or reproduced
in any manner whatsoever without written permission from the publisher except
in the case of brief quotations embodied in critical articles or reviews.
For information address Bloomsbury USA, 175 Fifth Avenue, New York, NY 10010.

For song lyric credits see final page.

Published by Bloomsbury USA, New York
Distributed to the trade by Macmillan

All papers used by Bloomsbury USA are natural, recyclable products made
from wood grown in well-managed forests. The manufacturing processes conform to
the environmental regulations of the country of origin.

LYBRARY OF CONGRESS CATALOGING-IN-PUBLICATION DATA HAS BEEN APPLIED FOR.

ISBN-10: 1-59691-476-9
ISBN-13: 978-1-59691-476-6

First U.S. Edition 2008

1 3 5 7 9 10 8 6 4 2

Printed in the United States of America by Quebecor World Fairfield

FOR MY FAMILY

"I THINK PEOPLE SHOULD JUST LISTEN TO IT,
THINK ABOUT IT, AND THEN MAKE UP THEIR OWN
MINDS AS TO WHAT IT SAYS TO THEM."
—FREDDIE MERCURY ON "BOHEMIAN RHAPSODY"

THE OTHER DAY, MY WIFE, ALIZA, AND I WENT TO SEE A TRIBUTE TO QUEEN AT THE BOWERY BALLROOM IN NEW YORK.

I DIDN'T KNOW WHAT TO EXPECT, SO AS A FAN, I WAS PSYCHED THAT THE BANDS* WERE PLAYING SOME PRETTY DEEP CUTS, AS WELL AS THE HITS.

YOU SUCK MY BLOOD LIKE A LEECH...

*IT WAS ACTUALLY ONE BAND AND ROTATING GUEST SINGERS

MY FRIEND ROB, WHOM I'VE KNOWN SINCE JUNIOR HIGH, WAS THERE TOO. HE'S A BIG QUEEN FAN AS WELL. I LIKE TO THINK THAT'S BECAUSE I PLAYED THEM SO MUCH BACK WHEN WE WERE KIDS.

I FELT REALLY EXCITED TO BE AT THE SHOW, BUT THE CROWD DIDN'T SEEM TO KNOW A LOT OF THE LYRICS, SO I FELT SELF-CONSCIOUS SINGING ALONG.

I WANT TO BREAK FREE FROM YOUR LIES—

I'M SURE THE AUDIENCE WAS HAVING FUN – BUT THEY DIDN'T SEEM TO GET REALLY ANIMATED UNTIL SOME OF THE MORE POPULAR SONGS WERE PLAYED.

AT ONE POINT ROB AND ALIZA WENT DOWNSTAIRS TO SEE SOME FRIENDS.

BII-CYCLE!

DON'T! STOP ME NOOOW...

THE SECOND ACT OPENED WITH "TIE YOUR MOTHER DOWN," FROM "A DAY AT THE RACES" (CURRENTLY MY FAVORITE QUEEN SONG). IT WAS SO AWESOME!

LATER ON, ROB AND ALIZA CAME BACK UPSTAIRS AND THE BAND PLAYED "FAT BOTTOMED GIRLS". THIS SONG REALLY SEEMED TO FINALLY EXCITE THE CROWD.

OF COURSE, "BOHEMIAN RHAPSODY" PUT THEM OVER THE TOP – DURING THE OPERATIC BIT YOU COULD TOTALLY FEEL THE ELECTRICITY BUILDING IN ANTICIPATION OF THE HARD-ROCKING CLIMAX.

"WAYNE'S WORLD" IS TOTALLY TO BLAME.

MY FRIEND ALEX ASKED ME LATER HOW QUEEN USED TO PERFORM THAT OPERA PART OF THE SONG LIVE IN CONCERT.

I TOLD HIM THAT I'D ALWAYS HEARD THEY'D PLAY A RECORDING AND LEAVE THE STAGE DURING THAT SECTION.

ALEX THOUGHT THAT WAS DUMB, BUT I DEFENDED QUEEN'S CHOICE. I KNOW IT JUST DOESN'T WORK TO TRY AND DO THAT LIVE. IT JUST SOUNDS STUPID.

IT WAS A FUN AND MEMORABLE NIGHT.

WHEN I THINK OF QUEEN I CAN REMEMBER MY WHOLE LIFE

WHEN I DECIDED TO WRITE A COMIC ABOUT MY OBSESSION WITH QUEEN, ONE OF THE FIRST MEMORIES THAT SPRUNG TO MIND WAS AN EVENING SPENT WITH MY GRANDPARENTS.

WHAT TIME IS IT ON THEN, MICHAEL?

SEVEN.

I THINK QUEEN IS STUPID.

IT WAS IN 1986, WHICH I KNOW FOR SURE BECAUSE WE WERE GOING TO WATCH A QUEEN CONCERT FROM THAT YEAR ON TV.

IT WOULDN'T HAVE BEEN LATER THAN THAT BECAUSE WE WERE STILL LIVING IN ENGLAND AT THE TIME.

SHUT UP! I THINK WHAM! IS STUPID!

SHUT UP, THEY ARE NOT!

I REMEMBER THAT MY DAD WAS GONE ALREADY TO AMERICA. HE HAD TO LEAVE AHEAD OF US TO GET THINGS ESTABLISHED.

MICHAEL! SARAH!

DON'T ARGUE!

HE HAD TO DO THINGS LIKE START HIS NEW JOB IN NEW YORK AND FIND A HOUSE FOR US TO LIVE IN WHEN WE GO OVER TOO.

ANYWAY, I DON'T LIKE ALL OF WHAM! I THINK ANDREW RIDGELEY IS UGLY.

I THINK YOU'RE UGLY.

MY MOTHER WAS OVER VISITING HIM FOR A WEEK, WHICH IS WHY MY GRANDPARENTS HAD COME DOWN FROM RUGBY TO BABYSIT.

I HATE YOU!!

The Ballad

UP NEXT IS A NEW ONE FROM A REAL BIG FAVE! IT'S "I WANT TO BREAK FREE" FROM QUEEN!!!

I WANT TO-BREAK FREE-EE

HAW HAW! LOOK AT THAT MAN, MUMMY!

YES, HE'S A FUNNY MAN, ISN'T HE, MICHAEL?

GOD KNOWS I WANT TO BREAK FREE.

I'VE FALLEN IN LO-OVE. I'VE FALLEN IN LOVE FOR THE FIRST TIME.

OHHH, HOW I WANT TO BREAK FREE-EE.

BUT LIFE STILL GOES ON...

OI, MICHAEL.

IT'S FANTASTIC! THE FIRST SONG, "DEATH ON TWO LEGS", IS REALLY LOUD!

OH, LET'S HEAR IT THEN.

IT MIGHT ANNOY THE NEIGHBOURS...

OH COME ON! PLAY IT!

OH, OKAY THEN.

I THINK THIS SONG IS GREAT.

YEAH, IT'S ALRIGHT.

BUT LIFE STILL GOES ON... I CAN'T GET USED TO LIVING WITHOUT, LIVING WITHOUT, YOOUU...

MICHAEL?

WHAT ARE YOU DOING?

THIS MAGAZINE'S GOT ALL THE WORDS TO "I WANT TO BREAK FREE" IN IT.

OH, LET ME SEE.

OOH, LOOK - IT'S GOT THE WORDS TO "EAT IT" AS WELL.

OI!

I'M LEARNING "I WANT TO BREAK FREE" BY HEART- SO CLEAR OFF!

SNATCH!

UP NEXT IS A LAD FROM LEIGHTON BUZZARD IN ENGLAND.

HANDS TOGETHER FOR MICHAEL DAWSON, AGED TEN.

CLAP CLAP

HERE YOU GO, SON.

THANKS!

THIS IS "BOHEMIAN RHAPSODY" BY QUEEN.

hff.

I—

VERY GOOD, VERY GOOD.

HANDS TOGETHER FOR MICHAEL AND "BOHEMIAN RHAPSODY."

CLAP CLAP

CLA CLA CL

THANK YOU, MICHAEL.

WELL THEN...

UP NEXT—

BUT I'M NOT FINISHED YET!!

YOU WHAT?

I'M NOT FINISHED YET!

THERE'S A WHOLE 'NOTHER VERSE.

OH?

HA HA HA HA

WELL...

I KNOW IT ALL BY HEART!

UM... WELL, CARRY ON THEN, I SUPPOSE...

I SEE A LITTLE SILHOU OF A M

BISMILLAH! NO!!
WE WILL NOT LET YOU GO!
LET HIM GOOOO!
BISMILLAH! WE WILL N
LET HIM GO! BISMI
WE WILL NOT LET YOU
LET HIM GO! WILL
LET ME GO!
WILL NOT LET YOU
LET ME GOOOO!

NO! NO! NO!

CLAP CLAP

WELL THEN, FOLKS - HANDS TOGETHER ONCE MORE FOR OUR MICHAEL AND HIS SINGING.

WASN'T HE JUST GRAND?

BUT!

BUT IT'S NOT FINISHED YET!

HA HA HA

NOW, MICHAEL -

I'M NOT DONE WITH THE SONG!

HA HA HA HA

ALRIGHT - IT STARTS OUT AT THIS BIG SCARY MOUNTAIN.

AMONGST THE ROCKS WE SEE A FIGURE.

THE MUSIC IS PLAYING AS HE STEPS FORWARD.

THEN HE PULLS OUT THIS GINORMOUS AXE AND HOLDS IT UP.

THEN - RIGHT BEFORE HE STARTS TO SING -

HE CHOPS REALITY IN HALF!!

SEE - HERE'S A DRAWING OF HIM AND HIS AXE.

VERY GOOD!

HULLO!

HULLO.

HELLO, DAD! I'M SHOWING MUMMY SOME DRAWINGS I DID FOR MY OWN MUSIC VIDEO.

OH, VERY GOOD.

HAVE YOU WRITTEN THE SONG YET?

NO, NOT YET.

HELLO, DADDY.

HULLO, SARAH.

SARAH, MICHAEL, COME AND SIT DOWN FOR TEA.

WHERE'S ANDREW?

HE'S OUT AT HIS FRIEND'S. HE'LL BE HOME SOON.

I WANTED TO ASK YOU BOTH IF YOU'D BEEN THINKING ABOUT WHAT WE'D TALKED ABOUT, GOING TO AMERICA.

UM...

I THINK IT'D BE GREAT TO MOVE TO AMERICA!

YEAH?

YOU LIKE THAT SONG THEN, DO YOU?

"BICYCLE RACE"? YEAH, IT'S GREAT. IT'S ON MY "QUEEN'S GREATEST HITS" ALBUM.

YEAH?

DOESN'T IT BOTHER YOU THAT FREDDIE MERCURY HATES "STAR WARS"?

huh?

HE DOESN'T HATE "STAR WARS"!

YES HE DOES. HE SAYS SO IN "BICYCLE RACE."

WHY WOULDN'T HE LIKE "STAR WARS"? "STAR WARS" IS BRILLIANT!!

HE SAYS HE DOESN'T LIKE SUPERMAN EITHER. WHAT DO YOU THINK ABOUT THAT?

AAAUGH!!

OH NO!! CLAIRE!! NO! I'M SORRY - I DIDN'T MEAN IT!!

DAD-DEEEEEE!

WAIT!

I'LL BUY YOU ANOTHER...

OOOH - WHAT HAPPENED?

I DUNNO - I JUST DROPPED IT - IT WAS AN ACCIDENT!

COME ON SARAH, LET'S GO INSIDE.

OI!

huh?

OI, YOU LITTLE GIT! I WANNA HAVE A WORD WITH YOU!!

I BOUGHT THIS BLOODY TOY FOR CLAIRE NOT TWO HOURS AGO AND ALREADY IT'S BROKEN!

DO YOU THINK I WORK ALL BLOODY WEEK JUST SO YOU CAN COME AROUND AND SMASH UP ALL MY THINGS?!!

DO YOU THINK IT'S FUNNY GOING AROUND BREAKING PEOPLE'S THINGS?!

DO YOU?!!

I...

um...

WHERE'S DADDY GOING?

PROBABLY TO HAVE A TALK WITH MR. REYNOLDS.

A FEW MINUTES LATER

MICHAEL! COME DOWN HERE!

MR. REYNOLDS WANTS TO HAVE A WORD WITH YOU.

HI MICHAEL, YEAH, I, uh... JUST WANTED TO, uh, SAY SORRY, YOU KNOW? FOR BEFORE?

I SHOULDN'T HAVE SHOUTED LIKE THAT.

IT WASN'T RIGHT.

SOMETIMES GROWN-UPS CAN HAVE ROUGH WEEKS, AND, uh..., CAN LOSE THEIR TEMPERS...

um... ANYWAY...

BOO HOO HOO!

A FEW MONTHS LATER

SOME TIME LATER

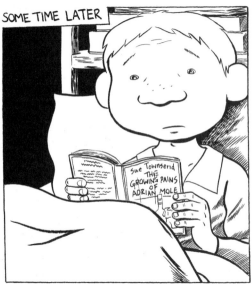

Sue Townsend
THE GROWING PAINS OF ADRIAN MOLE

HEY MICHAEL, I HEARD QUEEN' IS GOING TO BE AT MILTON KEYNES NEXT MONTH.

REALLY?!

THAT'S ONLY TWENTY MINUTES AWAY! MAYBE MUMMY WILL TAKE ME TO SEE THEM!

MAYBE.

"ASK HER ABOUT IT IN THE MORNING."

OKAY, LADS, LET'S DO IT ONE MORE TIME BEFORE WE GO ON.

I WANT TO BREAK FREE—

KNOCK KNOCK – SORRY BOYS – SORRY TO INTERRUPT, BUT THERE'S THIS LAD OUT FROM THE CROWD WHO WE THOUGHT MIGHT LIKE TO COME BACK AND SAY HELLO.

OH?

HELLO.

OH?

HELLO, MICHAEL – WOW, WHAT A GREAT T-SHIRT YOU'VE GOT ON.

WOW!! IT'S GREAT TO MEET YOU, FREDDIE MERCURY! I LOVE ALL YOUR SONGS!!

I'VE GOT FOUR OF YOUR ALBUMS, AND THIS T-SHIRT, AND I CAN SING "BOHEMIAN RHAPSODY" AND "I WANT TO BREAK FREE" BY HEART!! I ONCE DID "BOHEMIAN RHAPSODY" AT A TALENT CONTEST, AND EVERYONE THOUGHT IT WAS SO FUNNY!!

WOW, MICHAEL – YOU MUST BE OUR YOUNGEST FAN!! IT'S SO BRILLIANT THAT YOU CAME BACK HERE AND MADE FRIENDS WITH US.

WOW – HE KNOWS ALL OF THE WORDS...?!

THAT NOVEMBER, IN RUGBY, ENGLAND

OOH, I'M SO GLAD YOU MADE IT!

HELLO, GRANDMA.

HELLO, GRANDMA.

HI MUM.

COME IN, COME IN, GRANDAD'S JUST MAKING THE TEA.

SO...

GRANDMA- SARAH AND I ARE WORKING ON FORMING A ROCK BAND.

OOH, ISN'T THAT WONDERFUL?

SO, PAM, HOW'S DAVID GETTING ON IN AMERICA?

HE'S DOING WELL. HE'S GOT US A HOUSE IN NEW JERSEY.

OH AYE, WHAT'S NEW JERSEY LIKE, THEN?

HE'S RENTED A HOUSE IN A TOWN CALLED RED BANK. IT'S QUITE NEAR THE SEA. IT'S QUITE NICE ACTUALLY.

OH AYE.

WHAT'S THE NAME OF YOUR BAND, THEN, MICHAEL?

IMPERIAL DARKNESS.

HE REALLY HATED STAYING IN NEW YORK CITY.

THERE HE GOES - OFF TO EAT HIS TEA IN FRONT OF THE TELLY.

tch.

WE'VE DONE TWO SONGS.

SO "NEW JERSEY", eh?

WE SHOULD SHOW GRANDMA OUR SONGS LATER.

ALRIGHT.

YES.

WHAT ARE YOU GOING TO DO WITH THAT CAT OF YOURS?

QUEENIE?

IT'S NOT REALLY OUR CAT.

IT'S JUST A STRAY.

WELL, YOU'VE BEEN LOOKING AFTER IT. IT'S PRACTICALLY YOURS.

IS ANDREW GOING TO LOOK AFTER IT?

YOU'RE LEAVING HIM BEHIND, AFTER ALL.

NO, IT'S ALRIGHT, MUM, WE'RE LEAVING QUEENIE WITH SOME OF OUR OLD NEIGHBOURS.

I DIDN'T WANT TO CALL THE CAT "QUEENIE".

I THINK WE SHOULD HAVE CALLED IT "WHAMMY".

WELL, WE DIDN'T!

BECAUSE THAT'S A STUPID NAME!

ALRIGHT, NOW A WEREWOLF ATTACKS...

SORRY PAM, BUT

GRANDMA! GRANDMA! I DREW A WEREWOLF!

LOOK! LOOK!

MAYBE IN THE VIDEO SARAH CAN BE THE ONE WHO TURNS INTO A WEREWOLF.

WHAT DO YOU THINK OF THAT, SARAH? huh?

SEE, HERE'S ME, DRESSED LIKE FREDDIE MERCURY IN "I WANT TO BREAK FREE"

I DON'T KNOW...

AND YOU'RE THE CASIO PLAYER AND YOU GET TURNED, OK?

SO THERE'S THIS PART OF THE SONG WHERE

I JUST DON'T KNOW, MUM!

AND NOW YOU'VE SAID ALL THIS IN FRONT OF THE BLOODY KIDS!!

SLAM!

WELL!

AND SO FINALLY, DECEMBER 1986...

HEATHROW INT'L AIRPORT

SOME WEEKS LATER

OKAY, CLASS, WE'VE GOT A NEW STUDENT JOINING US TODAY.

LOOKIT...

THIS IS MICHAEL DAWSON.

HE'S FROM ENGLAND.

I REMEMBER STANDING IN FRONT OF THE CLASS AND BEING INTRODUCED.

I'M NOT SURE IF I WAS ACTUALLY WEARING A STRIPED SHIRT, THOUGH.

GUITAR

I KNOW I USED TO HAVE A STRIPED SWEATSHIRT. IT WAS BLUE AND WHITE, AND CAME WITH A PAIR OF MATCHING SWEATPANTS AND A HAN SOLO VEST.

I LOVED THIS OUTFIT - FOR SOME ODD REASON I THOUGHT IT MADE ME LOOK LIKE FREDDIE MERCURY FROM QUEEN.

CAN FACE ME

SOLO

SO I CAN EASILY IMAGINE MYSELF THINKING THAT THE OUTFIT WOULD BE PERFECT TO WEAR FOR MY FIRST DAY OF SCHOOL IN AMERICA.

BUT TRUTHFULLY I HAVE NO **REAL** MEMORY AT ALL OF WHAT I MIGHT HAVE HAD ON. THE ONLY ACTUAL MEMORY I HAVE IS STANDING UP AT THE FRONT OF A CLASSROOM WHILE A TEACHER EXPLAINED WHO I WAS.

I DON'T REALLY REMEMBER WHAT SHE LOOKED LIKE, THOUGH...

I KNOW I ONLY SPENT ONE DAY IN THAT CLASS. IT WAS FOURTH GRADE, AND AFTER A DAY SOMEBODY DETERMINED I WAS TOO OLD FOR IT.

IT'S SORT OF FUNNY TO ME THAT I WAS EVER PUT IN FOURTH GRADE AT ALL, BECAUSE EVEN WHEN I WAS BUMPED TO FIFTH GRADE I WAS STILL ALMOST OLD ENOUGH TO BE PUT INTO SIXTH.

BUT I KNOW WHY THAT HAPPENED — SOMEBODY HAD DECIDED THAT IT WOULD BE BEST FOR ME AND MY LITTLE SISTER IF WE STAYED IN THE SAME SCHOOL, AND SINCE SIXTH GRADE WAS MIDDLE SCHOOL, I WAS KEPT IN FIFTH.

IN FIFTH GRADE I LEARNED FOR THE FIRST TIME THAT THE UNITED STATES HAD ONCE BEEN A COLONY OF ENGLAND.

I REMEMBER THAT I WAS THE ONLY ONE WHO FELT THAT THE BRITISH HAD A RIGHT TO TAX THE AMERICAN COLONISTS.

I KNOW THAT I WAS ALONE IN THIS THOUGHT. I THINK THE TEACHER AND THE OTHER STUDENTS WERE PROBABLY DISGUSTED WITH ME. MY MEMORY OF IT IS FUZZY, THOUGH, LIKE ALL OF MY MEMORIES FROM THAT TIME.

MOST OF THE THINGS I RECALL FROM MY CHILDHOOD I CAN ONLY REMEMBER AS STATIC IMAGES. BLURRY PHOTOGRAPHS.

FOR EXAMPLE, MY MEMORY OF RUNNING DOWNSTAIRS TO SEE A MUSIC VIDEO BY BILLY JOEL LOOKS LIKE THIS:

ONE DAY AFTER SCHOOL I WAS BEATEN UP BY BULLIES - I REMEMBER IT LIKE THIS:

MY BIG BROTHER ANDREW SHOWED UP AND SCARED THEM AWAY LIKE THIS:

I REMEMBER BEING ON STAGE AT THE HOLIDAY CAMP AND SINGING "BOHEMIAN RHAPSODY" A CAPPELLA IN THE TALENT SHOW AND THINKING PEOPLE LOVED IT.

I REMEMBER MY DAD LEAVING FOR AMERICA AND SAYING GOODBYE TO US IN THE LIVING ROOM.

WHEN I WAS LITTLE I USED TO WORRY A LOT. LIKE MOST PEOPLE, I WORRIED MAINLY ABOUT NUCLEAR BOMBS AND WAR.

IN 1982, DURING THE BRIEF FALKLAND ISLANDS WAR BETWEEN BRITAIN AND ARGENTINA, I WAS CONVINCED MY THIR-TEEN-YEAR-OLD BROTHER WOULD BE DRAFTED.

I WORRIED MY PARENTS WOULD DIVORCE, OR THAT MY DAD WOULD LOSE HIS JOB, OR THAT SOMEONE MIGHT DIE, OR WHAT COULD BE AT THE EDGE OF THE UNIVERSE IF THE UNIVERSE WAS EVERYTHING THAT THERE IS, AND WHO WAS GOD'S DAD, AND SO ON...

AT SOME POINT I REALIZED THAT I DIDN'T HAVE ANY MEMORIES OF WHEN I WAS A BABY.

NONE WHATSOEVER FROM BETWEEN THE TIME I WAS BORN AND THE TIME I WAS ALREADY A FEW YEARS OLD. THE THOUGHT THAT MY MEMORIES COULD BE LOST FOREVER AND FORGOTTEN HAD ME VERY WORRIED.

IT WASN'T JUST THE MEMORIES THAT HAD ALREADY GONE - IT WAS THAT I MIGHT CONTINUE TO LOSE NEW ONES AS I AGED. I MIGHT EVENTUALLY FORGET MY WHOLE ENTIRE LIFE FOREVER.

THE REASON I CAN STILL REMEMBER BEING AFRAID OF LOSING MY MEMORIES IS BECAUSE I MADE A CONSCIOUS DECISION TO DO SO. I REMEMBER THE DAY I WAS THINKING ABOUT IT.

I WAS ON OUR STREET WITH SOMEONE, I THINK IT WAS MY MOM, BUT IT COULD HAVE BEEN SOMEONE ELSE. I KNOW WE WERE RUNNING TO GET A BUS.

IT HAD RAINED, AS IT DID A LOT IN ENGLAND, AND THE PATHS WERE WET.

I LOOKED DOWN AND SAW A PUDDLE WITH A PARTIALLY STEPPED-ON WORM SITTING HALFWAY IN IT.

AND I DECIDED THAT ANY TIME THAT I THOUGHT ABOUT MEMORY, I WOULD ALWAYS PICTURE THIS MOMENT FIRST.

AND BY DOING SO I WOULD ENSURE THAT I WOULD NEVER FORGET IT.

MY FIRST MEMORIES OF BEING IN AMERICA INCLUDE RIDING TO OUR NEW HOUSE FROM JFK AIRPORT IN THE BACK OF A VAN MY DAD HAD RENTED TO MOVE SOME SECOND-HAND FURNITURE, WHICH SMELLED NOT ENTIRELY UNPLEASANTLY LIKE A BASEMENT. OF COURSE, AT THAT TIME I DIDN'T YET KNOW WHAT BASEMENTS ACTUALLY WERE.

WHEN WE GOT TO THE HOUSE, "SWISS FAMILY ROBINSON" WAS ON TV. MY DAD HAD BOUGHT ME AND SARAH SOME FRUITY CEREAL FOR BREAKFAST. THE CEREAL WAS KIND OF GROSS, AND WE NEVER MANAGED TO FINISH THE BOX.

WHEN I WOKE UP THE NEXT MORNING AT 5:30 BECAUSE OF JET LAG, THE "RAMBO" CARTOON WAS ON, SO I WATCHED THAT.

SARAH AND I HAD THE TWO ROOMS UPSTAIRS. THERE WAS A PASSAGEWAY THAT WENT BETWEEN THEM BEHIND THE STAIRS, BUT WE WEREN'T ALLOWED TO GO THROUGH THERE IN CASE THE PREVIOUS TENANTS HAD LET A DOG POOP IN THERE.

WE HAD SOME SEVERE SNOWSTORMS THAT WINTER. IT WAS SHOCKING TO ME, BECAUSE IT HAD NEVER REALLY SNOWED QUITE AS MUCH AS THAT IN ENGLAND.

SARAH AND I WERE ALLOWED TO STAY HOME UNTIL JANUARY OF 1987, THEN WE HAD TO ENROLL IN SCHOOL.

WHEN I GOT TO AMERICA I WAS A LITTLE DISAPPOINTED TO DISCOVER THAT MY ADORABLE ACCENT DIDN'T MAKE ME AN INSTANT HIT WITH THE LADIES AND AN HONORARY MEMBER OF THE SCHOOL'S COOLER CLIQUES.

I THOUGHT, THOUGH, THAT I COULD SHOW THESE AMERICAN KIDS HOW COOL I COULD BE, AND THAT THE WAY TO DO IT WAS WITH MY FAVORITE POWDER-BLUE STRING VEST. FOR SOME REASON I HAD IT IN MY HEAD THAT STRING VESTS WERE STYLISH.

I WORE IT TO SCHOOL UNDER A SWEATER, PLANNING TO REVEAL IT LATER IN THE DAY. AFTER LUNCH I REMOVED MY SWEATER AND SHOWED THE OTHER KIDS EXACTLY HOW COOL I COULD BE.

IT TURNED OUT THAT STRING VESTS WERE NOT COOL IN AMERICA. I QUESTION IF THEY WERE REALLY THOUGHT OF AS STYLISH IN ENGLAND EITHER. I MIGHT HAVE JUST HAD THE WRONG IDEA ABOUT THEM.

THE OTHER KIDS' LAUGHTER LEFT ME WITH A BIT OF A DILEMMA. DID I ADMIT MY MISTAKE AND COVER BACK UP, OR DID I BRAZENLY LEAVE MY PASTY WHITE SKIN EXPOSED, EVEN IN THE FACE OF THEIR DERISION?

I DON'T REMEMBER HOW IT RESOLVED.

MAN, I LOVE TO TELL THAT STORY TO PEOPLE NOW. I DO IT BETTER IN PERSON, I HAVE ALL THE 'BEATS' ALL WORKED OUT, AS WELL AS SOME PANTOMIME IN THE KEY MOMENTS.

I WAS LISTENING TO TALK RADIO THE OTHER DAY WHILE I DREW. THE SHOW WAS ABOUT DIFFERENT PEOPLE'S THEORIES ABOUT WHAT IS A HUMAN SELF, OR WHAT IS IT THAT MAKES ME, ME?

ONE OF THE COMMENTATORS, HIS NAME WAS DAVID BROCK, CONFESSED HIS OWN DISBELIEF IN THE NOTION OF THE SELF AS A SOUL. WHEN ASKED, "THEN WHAT IS IT THAT MAKES YOU, YOU?", HE REPLIED, "THAT I TELL YOU A STORY."

HE WAS SAYING THAT THE THING THAT MAKES US BE US IS THE ONGOING NARRATIVE OF OUR LIFE THAT WE TELL TO OURSELVES. IT MADE ME THINK OF THE MOVIE "FIGHT CLUB," IN WHICH BRAD PITT'S CHARACTER INSISTS THAT "WE'RE NOT OUR JOBS, WE'RE NOT OUR CARS, WE'RE NOT OUR @#☆!! KHAKIS!"

I'VE ALWAYS HAD TO DISAGREE WITH BRAD, BECAUSE, WHILE NOBODY WANTS TO BE THEIR JOBS, THERE'S A LOT OF TRUTH IN THE FACT THAT WE ARE THE SUM OF ALL THE THINGS THAT HAVE HAPPENED TO US. IN SOME RESPECTS WE ARE WHAT WE DO.

EVERYTHING THAT'S HAPPENED TO US MAKES US WHO WE ARE. IF DIFFERENT THINGS HAD HAPPENED WE'D BE SOMEONE ELSE. WE'D HAVE DIFFERENT MEMORIES. DIFFERENT STORIES.

TRYING TO DRAW MEMORIES IS TRICKY, THEY'RE LIKE SOMETHING YOU CAN ONLY SEE IN YOUR PERIPHERAL VISION - THEY SEEM CONCRETE UNTIL YOU TRY TO LOOK DIRECTLY AT THEM IN ORDER TO RECREATE THE PICTURE IN YOUR MIND.

THEN THEY GET ALL FUZZY AND CRUMBLE

IN THE SUMMER WE WERE ABLE TO TAKE ADVANTAGE OF THE LAKE THAT THE HOUSE BACKED ONTO. WE SWAM AND CANOED.

I GUESS MY BROTHER MUST HAVE COME OVER TO STAY WITH US BY THEN, BECAUSE I REMEMBER HIM SWIMMING WITH US AND HIS GIRLFRIEND FROM ENGLAND WHO'D COME OVER WITH HIM.

I DON'T REMEMBER ANDREW LIVING WITH US PERMANENTLY IN AMERICA FOR A FEW YEARS. I KNOW HE CAME OVER AT ONE POINT AFTER FINISHING HIGH SCHOOL, BUT WENT BACK TO ENGLAND AFTER A LITTLE BIT BECAUSE HE DIDN'T LIKE IT.

HE WAS A LITTLE BIT OF A CURIOSITY TO SOME OF THE NEIGHBORHOOD FRIENDS I MADE, PROBABLY BECAUSE OF HIS U.K. ANARCHIST PUNK-ROCKER LOOK.

I KNOW HE MUST HAVE BEEN HERE IN 1989 BECAUSE I REMEMBER BEING IN A RECORD STORE WITH HIM AND TALKING ABOUT THE NEW QUEEN ALBUM THAT HAD JUST COME OUT, "THE MIRACLE".

QUEEN WASN'T ON THE NEWS IN THE U.S. VERY MUCH, SO I DIDN'T KNOW WHAT WAS HAPPENING WITH THEM. ANDREW SAID PEOPLE IN ENGLAND THOUGHT FREDDIE MERCURY WAS GETTING FAT IN HIS OLD AGE.

"THE MIRACLE" IS MY LEAST FAVORITE QUEEN ALBUM

THE FIRST TIME I EVER WENT TO NEW YORK I WAS SO SCARED I WAS ALMOST CRYING. I KEPT ASKING IF WE COULD GO BACK TO THE CAR AND GO HOME.

THE CITY IS ABOUT AN HOUR'S DRIVE OR SO FROM RED BANK. I THINK WE MUST HAVE DRIVEN BECAUSE I THINK I REMEMBER MY DAD GETTING A TICKET AT THE END OF THE DAY.

I WAS TERRIFIED THAT WE'D BE SHOT AND KILLED AT ANY MOMENT AS WE WALKED AROUND THE CITY.

I BLAME IT ON THE NIGHTLY NEWS...

CONNIE CHUNG

...TRAGEDY TONIGHT IN THE BRONX AS THREE MEN, RU-

WE WENT UP TO THE TOP OF THE WORLD TRADE CENTER AND I WAS NERVOUS ABOUT STANDING TOO CLOSE TO THE GLASS ON THE OBSERVATION DECK.

I USED TO BE SCARED OF LIGHTNING TOO. I DON'T KNOW WHAT WAS THE MATTER WITH ME THAT I WAS SUCH A LITTLE WUSS. IT'S EMBARRASSING.

THAT SAME RADIO SHOW HAD ANOTHER PART IN WHICH THEY WERE DISCUSSING HOW THE HUMAN MIND SETS ITSELF APART FROM THE OTHER ANIMALS.

IT BROKE DOWN SOMETHING LIKE THIS: A CREATURE LIKE A WORM HAS NO MENTAL SENSE OF ITS "SELF," OR OF THE THINGS THAT SURROUND IT.

REMEMBER WHAT
LIKE, THOUGH...

IT DOESN'T KNOW WHAT A PUDDLE IS, OR WHAT A SIDEWALK IS. IT CAN'T IMAGINE OR TELL ITSELF THE STORY OF WHAT THESE THINGS ARE. IT JUST REACTS TO IMMEDIATE SENSORY INPUT.

OTHER ANIMALS CAN IMAGINE THE WORLD AROUND THEM AND EVEN SOMEWHAT INTERPRET IT. LIKE A CAT CAN KNOW WHAT CAT FOOD IS, AND CAN UNDERSTAND WHAT THE SOUND OF A CAN OPENER OPENING A CAN MEANS.

QUEEENIE ♪ ♫
TEA-
TIME ♪

BUT HUMANS ARE THE ONLY ANIMALS WHO CAN TELL THEMSELVES THE STORY OF THINGS THAT COULD NEVER EXIST.

SO IT'S UNLIKELY THAT THAT WORM HAS ANY MEMORY OF ME THE WAY THAT I HAVE A MEMORY OF IT.

I WENT DOWN TO RED BANK TO VISIT MY PARENTS RECENTLY, AND I LET THEM READ WHAT I HAD OF "FREDDIE & ME."

MY DAD TOLD ME THAT THE NEIGHBOR WHO'D YELLED AT ME WHEN I BROKE HIS DAUGHTER'S "PEEPER KEYPER" WAS APPARENTLY DRUNK AT THE TIME.

HE SAID THAT WHEN HE WENT OVER THERE TO SORT THE GUY OUT FOR YELLING, HE SEEMED REALLY OUT OF IT AND HIS WIFE LOOKED EMBARRASSED.

I WONDER WHAT MY DAD'S MENTAL SNAPSHOTS OF THE INCIDENT ARE.

I KNOW WHAT THE BLURRY PHOTOGRAPH IN MY MIND LOOKS LIKE...

I WONDER WHAT'S INSIDE MY DAD'S...

WHAT'S THE MEMORY THAT THE FOURTH-GRADE TEACHER HAS OF ME COMING INTO HER CLASS FOR A DAY?

DOES MY MOTHER HAVE A SNAPSHOT IN HER MIND OF ME RUNNING DOWN-STAIRS TO SEE QUEEN ON THE TELLY?

THUMP
THUMP
THUMP

DOES THAT BULLY REMEMBER THIS?

ANDREW?

THE AUDIENCE?

DAD?

The Opera

I WAS ACTUALLY SURPRISED TO HEAR IN THE RADIO BROADCAST THAT HE WAS GAY.

I DUNNO MAYBE THAT MAKES ME KINDA NAIVE.

BUT IN MY DEFENSE IT WASN'T ANYTHING HE'D ADMITTED PREVIOUSLY.

THEY SAID HE WAS GAY TOO.

YEAH.

AND IT'S NOT LIKE HE'S THE ONLY ROCK STAR I CAN THINK OF WHO DRESSES UP ALL FLAMBOYANTLY AND KIND OF ANDROGYNOUSLY.

I MEAN, MY FRIEND NEIL HAD A POSTER OF POISON ON HIS WALL WHERE THEY ALL LOOKED LIKE WOMEN, AND THEY'RE NOT GAY.

NOT THAT IT REALLY MAKES A DIFFERENCE TO ME AND ALL MY FRIENDS. WE'RE ANTI-PREJUDICE AND NON-CONFORMIST, SO WE DON'T HAVE PROBLEMS WITH GAYS.

I MEAN, SOMETIMES ME AND ROB CALL EACH OTHER FAGS, BUT WE ONLY MEAN IT IN A JOKING WAY.

HI MIKE!

HEY, WHAT'S UP?

THIS IS MY GIRLFRIEND, ALEXANDRIA.

SHE'S A FRESHMAN, A YEAR YOUNGER THAN I AM.

SHE USED TO DATE MY FRIEND PETAR.

HE SAYS HIS FAVORITE BAND IS ZZ TOP, BUT I THINK HE JUST SAYS THAT BECAUSE HE DOESN'T REALLY HAVE A PARTICULAR FAVE.

ALEX IS INTO THAT "ALTERNATIVE" TYPE OF MUSIC - LIKE NIRVANA AND THEM.

IN PARTICULAR, SHE LIKES NED'S ATOMIC DUSTBIN AND BIG AUDIO DYNAMITE.

OF COURSE, I DON'T LIKE THAT STUFF, AND I ALSO THINK IT'S STUPID THAT THEY CALL IT "ALTERNATIVE" MUSIC, SINCE IT'S ALL YOU EVER HEAR PLAYED ON THE RADIO.

THAT'S WHAT ROB'S BROTHER MARTIN SAYS.

HE'S MAD BECAUSE HE'S A MUSICIAN, AND HIS BAND PLAYS ROCK AND ROLL - AND ALL ANYONE WANTS TO HEAR ANYMORE IS "ALTERNATIVE". HE ALSO SAYS ALL THOSE ALTERNATIVE MUSICIANS CAN'T PLAY THEIR INSTRUMENTS EITHER. ROB'S BROTHER IS A PRETTY AWESOME GUITARIST.

I DON'T LIKE ALTERNATIVE MUSIC BECAUSE I LIKE TO LISTEN TO SINGERS THAT CAN ACTUALLY SING.

WHO'S THIS?

"DISCUSS MAN"?

WHAT ARE HIS POWERS?

SUPER DISCUSSIONS?

NO! IT'S DISCUS MAN!!

DISCUS - LIKE ONE YOU THROW.

HE CAN RIDE AROUND ON THEM AND THROW THEM.

OH, I THOUGHT MAYBE HE HAD SPECIAL TALKING POWERS OR SOMETHING.

SHUT UP, ROB!

OH, TIME FOR HOMEROOM.

BRRIIING!

I THINK MY X-L FORCE COMIC IS PRETTY GOOD.

I BETTER GET GOING ON IT, THOUGH. IT'S DUE IN A WEEK.

HEY MIKE.

OH, HEY, ORION.

HEY, MIKE - I WAS SORRY TO HEAR ABOUT FREDDIE MERCURY.

ORION IS A YEAR OLDER THAN ME.

YEAH, IT SUCKS.

YEAH, I HOPE HE STILL LIVES FOR A FEW YEARS.

I KNOW HIM FROM BEING IN SCHOOL PLAYS.

YEAH, ME TOO.

HE'S A BIG QUEEN FAN TOO.

I LIKE TO THINK HE'S A FAN BECAUSE OF ME.

I THINK IT'S FAIR TO SAY I'VE INTRODUCED A LOT OF MY FRIENDS TO QUEEN.

PLED
ALL

MAGIC?

WELL

WHEN I FIRST GOT HERE NOBODY WAS A FAN.

ROB AND ORION PROBABLY LIKE THEM THE MOST. NEXT TO ME, OF COURSE.

SET!

89

MOST AMERICANS I KNOW SEEM TO ONLY KNOW QUEEN FROM "ANOTHER ONE BITES THE DUST" AND "UNDER PRESSURE".

THE BIOL
OF TH

GEORGE MICHAEL IS DEFINITELY POPULAR HERE, THOUGH.

THE FUNCTION O
THE VERTICAL

HIS STUPID "FAITH" SONG WAS HUGE AND "I WANT YOUR SEX" WAS VOTED SONG OF THE YEAR BY MY EIGHTH-GRADE CLASS.

NOW HE'S MAKING VIDEOS WHERE HE REFUSES TO APPEAR IN THEM.

HA HA - I KNOW THAT MAKES SARAH MAD! SHE'S STILL IN LOVE WITH HIM.

THE NEXT MORNING.

MICHAEL?

IT WAS JUST ON THE RADIO -

FREDDIE MERCURY'S DIED.

THIS IS EMBARRASSING.

OKAY, OKAY.

ALRIGHT.

ALRIGHT.

PULL YOURSELF TOGETHER!

COME ON!

OH, FOR CHRIST'S SAKE!

THIS IS RETARDED!

COME ON, COME ON!

DON'T!

DON'T!

gkh!

GOD! WHAT A FUCKING BABY!!

UM...

MRS. HARTNETT?

CAN I GO TO THE NURSE?

I'M GLAD THAT WILLIE AND I CAN BE FRIENDS, AND DO THINGS, AND ROB DOESN'T GET ALL POSSESSIVE OF HER LIKE ALEX DOES WITH ME.

HE'S LUCKY TO HAVE A FUN GIRLFRIEND LIKE HER.

HE'S LUCKY THAT HIS GIRLFRIENDS MAKE OUT WITH HIM MORE THAN MINE DO WITH ME, TOO!

WE WENT ON A DOUBLE DATE TO SEE "HOOK". ROB AND WILLIE WERE GOING TOGETHER LIKE CRAZY! I HAD TO SHIELD ALEX FROM SEEING!

WHY AM I SO UPSET ABOUT THE DEATH OF FREDDIE MERCURY?!

EMPTY SPACES

WHAT ARE WE LIVING FOR?

SOON AFTER FREDDIE DIED, QUEEN ANNOUNCED THEY WERE BREAKING UP.

THIS WAS A DOUBLE BLOW TO ME.

ABANDONED PLACES

QUEEN WILL BE SORELY MISSED.

NOW WE ARE LEFT WITH NOTHING EXCEPT FOR THIS ROT CALLED DANCE MUSIC. CRUD LIKE C+C MUSIC FACTORY, COLOR ME BADD AND THE DEVIL HIMSELF, VANILLA ICE.

FREDDIE MERCURY IS (AS IN HIS NAME) A MESSENGER FROM THE GODS TO SPREAD GOOD MUSIC.

I GUESS WE KNOOW THE SCORE

I NEED A FRIEND LIKE WILLIE BY MY SIDE AS I GO THROUGH THIS. I DON'T CARE WHAT ALEX THINKS!

SWEET SIXTE

ISN'T IT COOL?

I GOT IT AT THE TUXEDO STORE UP THE TOWN.

YEAH!

I'M GOING TO BUY SOME SPATS FOR MY SHOES TOO.

YOU'VE GOT SO MUCH STYLE!

HA HA!

ROB!

EW!

COME ON, MIKE—LET'S GO STICK THIS ON NEIL!

HAHA OKA

SWEET SIXTEEN

♫ STRAIGHT UP ♫

DON'T ♫ WORRY BEEE H

BLAME IT ON ♫ THE RAA ♫

AS ♫ ICE

WILLING TO SAC-RI ♫ ♫

MAMA ♫ ♫

OOOOO

JUST KILLED A MAAANN ♫♫

PUT MY GUN AGAINST HIS HEEEAAD ♫ ♫

PULLE... NOW HE'S DEADD ♪ ♪

MA... ...OO... DIDN'T MEAN TO MAKE YOU CRY ♫

IF... NO... B... ♪

MIKE?

CARRY... ♪ CARRY...

MIKE?

...O REAL

MIKE?

ARE YOU OKAY, MIKE?

I WONDER WHAT EVERYONE THOUGHT OF ME DOING THAT.

I THINK ALEX WAS EMBARRASSED.

I BET EVERYONE COULDN'T BELIEVE WHAT A BIG QUEEN FAN I WAS...

I DUMPED ALEX A LITTLE WHILE AFTER THAT.

IT JUST WASN'T MEANT TO BE.

WHAT HAVE YOU COME UP WITH, MICHAEL?

WHAT HAVE YOU GOT THERE?

MISS PRISCO IS TEACHING US HOW TO DO SILK-SCREENING.

WELL...

IT'S LIKE A TRIBUTE...

NOW THAT I'VE DRAWN MY PICTURE, I HAVE TO CUT OUT A TRACING OF IT IN PLASTIC WITH A SCALPEL.

IT TAKES A LONG TIME.

IT'S GOING TO BE AWESOME.

NOW THAT I'VE BROKEN UP WITH ALEX, I HAVE TO THINK ABOUT GETTING ANOTHER GIRLFRIEND.

THERE ARE DEFINITELY SOME GIRLS IN SCHOOL THAT I LIKE-LIKE.

I KNOW ROB HAS A BETTER "LOVE LIFE" THAN I DO, BUT I THINK SOME GIRLS THINK I'M CUTE TOO.

I THINK SOME GIRLS THINK I'M FUNNY. I KNOW WILLIE THINKS I'M HILARIOUS. SO I HAVE THAT.

THE OTHER DAY I WAS OVER ROB'S AND HE AND WILLIE WERE MAKING OUT LIKE I WASN'T EVEN THERE.

I WISH HE WOULDN'T BOTHER INVITING ME OVER IF HE'S PLANNING ON HAVING HIS GIRLFRIEND OVER AS WELL.

THE ONLY REASON I'M INVITED HALF THE TIME IS SO HIS PARENTS DON'T THINK HE'S DOING ANYTHING.

I THINK THAT'S SELFISH.

THIS CAME OUT GOOD!

THAT DOES LOOK NICE - IS YOUR SCREEN FOR THE FRONT READY TO GO?

YEAH.

I'M SO EXCITED ABOUT MY TRIBUTE T-SHIRT!

IT'S GOING TO BE SO COOL TO WEAR AROUND SCHOOL NEXT WEEK.

Queen

Freddie Mercury 1946-1991

MAN, I'VE JUST BEEN THINKING—WHAT MR. LYNN SAID IN ENGLISH CLASS—MAYBE IT WOULD BE A GOOD EXPERIENCE TO JUST TAKE OFF FOR A WHILE...

YOU KNOW—JUST GET OUT OF HERE—GO ON THE ROAD...

JUST LIVE A LITTLE, RIGHT?

HEY, IS THAT TAPE OVER?

I BROUGHT THIS QUEEN MIX.

OH COOL.

CASSETTE

SHE'S A FAIRY FELL-ER

IS THIS SONG ABOUT D&D?

IT'S ABOUT FAIRIES.

YEAH, IT'S OFF "QUEEN II."

MY FAVORITE QUEEN ALBUM, I THINK.

THAT'S THE COOL THING ABOUT QUEEN— THEY'VE GOT SONGS FOR ALL OCCASIONS.

YEAH, THEY'RE REALLY ECLECTIC, YOU KNOW?

YOU KNOW WHICH QUEEN SONG IS DUMB?

"DON'T TRY SUICIDE."

IT'S NOT DUMB, IT'S A GOOD SONG.

NAH, IT'S DUMB. ME AND MY BROTHER ARE ALWAYS MAKING FUN OF IT.

heh

I'M GOING OUTSIDE FOR A MINUTE.

OH, OK

OKAY

WHO GAVE FREDDIE MERCURY AIDS?

WHO GAVE MAGIC JOHNSON AIDS?

WERE THEY THE SAME PERSON?

THE ANSWERS TO THESE QUESTIONS WILL PROBABLY NEVER BE KNOWN.

I WANT TO KNOW WHO IT WAS WHO KILLED MY IDOL.

I DO NOT HATE THEM, AS THEY MAY BE DEAD, OR STILL SUFFERING.

I JUST WISH IF THEY HAD KNOWN ABOUT THEIR DISEASE THEY HAD KEPT IT TO THEMSELVES.

FUCKING ROB!

IT'S LIKE EVERYTHING HIS BROTHER SAYS IS LIKE THE WORD OF GOD!

DO YOU WANT TO TALK ABOUT IT, MIKE?

I JUST FEEL SUCH A SENSE OF LOSS...

ANYONE WANT TO GO GET A CUP OF COFFEE?

I'M SO LONELY...

YOU GUYS ARE SO LUCKY THAT YOU HAVE EACH OTHER.

YOU'LL FIND SOMEONE.

YEAH, YOU'RE A GREAT CATCH!

REALLY?

YOU THINK SO?

I COULD GO FOR A CUP OF COFFEE.

OKAY.

IF I REALLY TOOK OFF AND GOT OUT OF TOWN—

WOULD YOU GUYS COME WITH ME?

uhh... I DUNNO...

ARE YOU REALLY THINKING ABOUT RUNNING AWAY FROM HOME?

I AM.

I'M REALLY SERIOUS ABOUT DOING IT!

I HAVE A LITTLE BIT OF MONEY...

LIKE $300.

I COULD GET TO FLORIDA ON THAT...

YOUR ENGLISH TEACHER REALLY SUGGESTED YOU ALL RUN AWAY FROM HOME?

HE DID, YEAH.

HE EVEN EXPLAINED HOW TO GET HOME FOR FREE BY TURNING OUR-SELVES IN TO MISSING CHILDREN.

ISN'T THIS GOING TO UPSET EVERYONE'S PARENTS?

HE SAID THEY'D EVENTUALLY GET OVER IT.

HE SAID IT'D BECOME A STORY IN OUR "FAMILY MYTHOLOGIES".

IT WOULD BE GOOD TO JUST GET OUT OF HERE, Y'KNOW?

YOU SHOULD TOTALLY COME! IT'D BE SUCH AN EXPERIENCE!

WE COULD JUST SLEEP ON THE BEACHES.

I LIKE HANGING OUT WITH NEIL BECAUSE HE LIKES DRAWING TOO.

WE BOTH LIKE DRAWING OUR OWN SUPERHERO COMICS.

WE BOTH REALLY LOVE THE X-MEN.

ESPECIALLY ANYTHING DONE BY JOHN BYRNE.

THIS IS THEIR BEST ALBUM.

"MOVING PICTURES."

NEIL'S FAVORITE BANDS USED TO BE WARRANT AND POISON, BUT NOW HE LOVES RUSH.

I LIKE SOME OF WHAT HE'S PLAYED ME. THE LEAD SINGER HAS A PRETTY GOOD VOICE.

MY FAVORITE SONG BY THEM IS CALLED "THE TEMPLES OF SYRINX". IT'S FROM A CONCEPT ALBUM CALLED "2112".

NEIL SAYS IT'S BASED ON A BOOK CALLED "ANTHEM", BY AYN RAND.

I GUESS I LIKE RUSH ALRIGHT.

RUSH

HERE - LET ME FAST-FORWARD THIS SONG - "LIMELIGHT" IS REALLY GOOD TOO.

uh...

DO YOU WANT TO MAYBE TRY AND RECORD SOMETHING?

oh, OK.

I HAVE TWO SETS OF LYRICS THAT I WROTE.

COOL.

OKAY, THE FIRST ONE IS A RAP. IT'S CALLED "CHEEL, WAZZUP?"

IF YA COME AT ME THEN I'LL KNOCK YA DOWN - IF YA FRONT WIT' ME YOU'LL EAT DA GROUND-

'COS I'M A KILL BOY, A HILL BOY, A LIL' BOY, A THRILL BOY-

COOL OFF YOUR JETS AN' LEARN HOW TA CHILL BOYYEEEE

CHEEL WAZZUP?

CHEEEEL, WAZZ UP?!

NEIL AND I ARE STARTING OUR OWN BAND.

WE'RE GOING TO CALL OURSELVES "IMPERIAL DARKNESS."

I THOUGHT YOU DIDN'T LIKE RAP.

I DON'T, REALLY - IT WAS JUST AN IDEA. MY OTHER SONG IS A ROCK SONG.

DON'T YOU THINK THOSE ARE PRETTY GOOD LYRICS?

I'M GOING TO BE THE LEAD SINGER.

NEIL IS ON THE DRUMS.

YEAH, THEY WERE' GOOD.

IMPERIAL DARKNESS

PRETTY AWESOME, RIGHT?

IT'S ONLY GOT ONE SONG RECORDED ON IT SO FAR, BUT ME AND NEIL HAVE OTHERS.

CAN I BORROW IT?

RIINNG!

uh, SURE.

JUST BE CAREFUL WITH IT.

YEAH, I WILL.

WHO'S "SWEELY B."?

THAT'S NEIL'S STAGE NAME.

I'M "DJ MASTER MIKE."

OH, I SEE.

ALRIGHT, SEE YOU AT LUNCH.

OKAY.

WHAT HAVE YOU GOT NEXT?

ART CLASS WITH MISS PRISCO

HAVE YOU STARTED YOUR TWENTY-HOUR PROJECT, MICHAEL?

YEAH, I'M WELL INTO IT NOW, MISS PRISCO.

MY NEW IDEA FOR A TWENTY-HOUR PROJECT IS MUCH BETTER THAN MY ONE FROM LAST TIME.

YOU SEE, I'M ADAPTING THE SONG "BOHEMIAN RHAPSODY" BY QUEEN INTO A COMIC.

OH?

IT'S REALLY CLEVER.

IT MAKES SENSE RIGHT? I MEAN, THE LYRICS OBVIOUSLY TELL A STORY.

IT'S PERFECT TO ADAPT INTO A COMIC.

I DON'T THINK THAT ANYONE'S EVER MADE A COMIC LIKE THIS.

IT'S ALL ABOUT THIS BIG MURDER TRIAL, SEE?

THIS IS THE GUY WHO KILLS SOMEONE.

AND THEN, uh, THERE'S GOING TO BE THESE JUDGES WHO, uh, PUT HIM ON TRIAL - THEY'RE GOING TO BE KIND OF, um, SUPERNATURAL...

WELL, THAT LOOKS INTERESTING, MIKE...

AND THEN AFTER, HE, uh, GETS REAL MAD AND HE, uh, YELLS AT EVERYONE...

I REALLY THINK THIS IS THE BEST IDEA I'VE EVER HAD AS AN ARTIST.

SO...

WHAT HAVE WE GOT HERE?

IT'S A STILL LIFE.

YOU'VE GOT EXCELLENT CONTROL OVER THE COLOR.

THANKS, THIS IS PART OF A SERIES.

WELL, I THINK THAT'S WONDERFUL.

THANKS, MISS PRISCO.

THAT STILL-LIFE DRAWING IS ALRIGHT, I GUESS.

CAN'T MISS PRISCO SEE THAT MY PROJECT IS BETTER, THOUGH?

CAN'T SHE SEE THAT MINE JUST HAS SO MUCH MORE MEANING?

IT'S SO ANNOYING, EVER SINCE "WAYNE'S WORLD" IT'S NOW COOL ALL OF A SUDDEN TO LIKE QUEEN.

EVERYBODY THINKS IT'S SO MUCH FUN TO SING "BOHEMIAN RHAPSODY" - IT'S ALL OVER THE DUMB POP STATIONS LIKE Z-100.

THE VIDEO WAS NUMBER TWO ON MTV'S MOST WANTED COUNTDOWN YESTERDAY AFTERNOON.

EVEN WORSE, THEY'VE GONE AND CHANGED THE VIDEO NOW SO IT'S GOT ALL THESE CLIPS FROM "WAYNE'S WORLD" IN IT. UGH!!

ARGH!!

IT MAKES ME SO MAD!

I'm just a poor boy

SO ANYWAY, LIKE I SAID, IN MY COMIC THERE'S A GUY WHO KILLED SOMEONE.

HE HAS TO GO ON TRIAL AND HIS MOTHER IS REALLY UPSET ABOUT IT.

I THINK HE LOOKS BEST IN HIS DIAMOND SPANDEX OUTFIT.

SO HE'S TAKEN BEFORE THE JUDGES.

AND HE PLEADS HIS CASE AND ASKS FOR MERCY.

THE JUDGES ARGUE OVER THE DECISION.

ONE OF THEM SAYS TO LET THE BOY GO.

BUT HE IS OVERWHELMED BY A MORE FORCEFUL JUDGE.

THEY FIND HIM GUILTY!!

AND HE IS CAST INTO HELL!

BUT, BEFORE HE VANISHES, HE FINDS THE STRENGTH TO TURN TO THE CROWD TO CAST HIS OWN JUDGMENT ON THEM —

I WONDER IF THEY WOULD EVER MAKE A MOVIE ABOUT FREDDIE MERCURY.

ASIDE FROM HIM BEING IN QUEEN, I DON'T KNOW THAT MUCH ABOUT HIM.

I DON'T KNOW IF HIS LIFE WAS INTERESTING ENOUGH TO BE MADE INTO A FILM.

SO, WHAT ARE YOU AND ROB GETTING UP TO TONIGHT?

I DUNNO, PROB'LY JUST HANGING OUT.

OKAY, BYE MUM!

GOODNIGHT! HAVE FUN!

HEY MIKE.

HEY ROB.

MAYBE TRY JUMPING INTO THE PIPE BEHIND THE CANNONS?

mm.

YO!! IS THAT MIKE DAWSON IN THERE?!

?

?

YO! LOOK WHO IT IS!

HEY DUDE!

FUCKING AWESOME DEMO TAPE YOU MADE THERE!!

IT'S ROB'S BROTHER.

heh heh

THAT RAT-KILLER SONG?! MAN, THAT'S DESTINED TO BE A HEAVY METAL CLASSIC!

HA HA!

HA HA! ♪ RAT-KILL-ERRR-BLOOD THIRSTY MAD-MAN ♪

HA HA HA!

OH MAN!

I WAS LAUGHING SO HARD WHEN ROB PLAYED ME THAT!

HA HA - IT'S SO GREAT HOW "SCARY" THE SONG IS!

I LOVE NEIL "ON THE PENCILS"!

HA HA HA!

HAR!

OHH SHIT!! THAT'S FUNNY!

SO... WHAT ARE YOU TWO LOSERS UP TO TONIGHT?

UM...

NUTHIN'

MAN, YOU TWO HAVE 'GOT' TO GET LIVES! IT'S FRIDAY NIGHT!

OKAY, I'M GOING OUT.

LATER ON, "DJ MASTER MIKE"!

SHUT

JERK!

THEY'LL BE SORRY...

YOU KNOW THIS BAND WAS MOSTLY NEIL'S IDEA, NOT MINE, RIGHT?

ROB AND WILLIE BROKE UP A FEW WEEKS AGO.

THE DAY AFTER, ROB WAS WANDERING AROUND SCHOOL ALL DEPRESSED AND CRYING.

I THINK HE OPENS UP TO PEOPLE TOO MUCH, HE TELLS PEOPLE PERSONAL THINGS ABOUT HIMSELF THAT THEY REALLY DON'T NEED TO KNOW.

SOMETIMES HE GETS ME SO ANNOYED!!

I'VE BEEN SO WRAPPED UP IN HIS PROBLEMS LATELY, I FORGOT THAT IT'S BEEN A LONG TIME SINCE I'VE BEEN WITH A GIRL.

MICHAEL! WILLIE'S HERE, COME AND LET HER IN!

OKAY MOM!

HI!

HEY – WHAT'S UP?

OOH, IS THAT YOUR DIARY?

CAN I READ IT?

No WAY!

IT'S _PRIVATE_!

HA HA!

DO YOU WRITE ABOUT THE GIRLS YOU "LIKE"?

MAYBE, BUT YOU'LL NEVER KNOW...

OH, COME ON! WHO DO YOU LIKE?

OH, I DON'T KNOW... MEGHAN MAYBE...

OOOH! YOU LIKE MEGHAN!

DO YOU KEEP A DIARY?

NO, NOT REALLY.

I WROTE A PLAY ONCE... ABOUT ME AND ROB.

OH, CAN I READ THAT?

EH, I DUNNO.

WHAT'S THIS?

OH, THIS IS FROM MY X-L FORCE COMIC I'M DOING FOR ART CLASS.

WHO'S THAT A DRAWING OF?

HER NAME'S "FLASHLIGHT". SHE'S TELEKINETIC AND TELEPATHIC.

I THINK YOU DREW HER BOOBS WRONG. THEY'RE TOO HIGH UP IN HER ARMPITS.

DID I?

I'M NOT SO GOOD AT DRAWING WOMEN...

DO YOU STILL THINK YOU'LL BE AN ARTIST WHEN YOU GROW UP?

OH, DEFINITELY.

I'LL NEVER BE SOME SOULLESS DRONE STUCK IN SOME OFFICE.

I DUNNO IF I'LL EVEN GO TO COLLEGE.

YOU DON'T NEED TO IF YOU WANT TO BE AN ARTIST.

OF COURSE I'LL PROBABLY SPEND A YEAR LIVING ABROAD SOMEWHERE...

HAVE YOU EVER THOUGHT OF DESIGNING A TATTOO FOR YOURSELF?

OH YEAH- DEFINITELY.

I'M GOING TO GET ONE.

WHAT WILL YOU GET?

I THINK A "LION RAMPANT" - THE SYMBOL OF SCOTLAND.

I'D GET A HUGE ONE EMBLAZONED ACROSS MY BACK.

WITH FIRE GOING DOWN MY SHOULDERS AND UP MY NECK.

THAT SOUNDS REALLY COOL!

YEAH, I CAN'T WAIT TO GET IT.

YOU SHOULD DRAW IT ON MY BACK.

DO YOU THINK YOU COULD?

THE TATTOO?

YEAH!

YOU HAVE THESE MARKERS HERE—CAN YOU DRAW IT?

IT WOULD BE COOL!

SO...

IT'S GREAT YOU'VE GOT A TALENT, MIKE.

YEAH, IT'S COOL.

I'VE BEEN LISTENING TO FREDDIE MERCURY'S SOLO SONG "THE GREAT PRETENDER."

ART CLASS

OFTENTIMES I FEEL LIKE THIS SONG IS ABOUT ME.

WITH HIM TOO.

OH YEAH?

IT'S ABOUT A MAN WHO APPEARS TO BE HAPPY BUT HAS MANY SECRET LONGINGS.

WELL I JUST DON'T KNOW. I THINK SHE MUST BE BIPOLAR, YOU KNOW?

mm.

ARE YOU FINISHED?

CAN I SEE?

THAT'S SO COOL!

MICHAEL, IT'S TIME FOR TEA - IT'S TIME FOR WILLIE TO GO HOME NOW.

OKAY MOM!

"TIME FOR TEA."

HA HA!

OKAY, SEE YOU TOMORROW.

LOOK. I WATCH BOTH SHOWS, SO I'M UNBIASED, BUT "STAR TREK" IS A MUCH BETTER SERIES!

NO WAY!

DU DON'T KNOW WHAT KING ABOUT!

NO DUDE, YOU'RE "QUANTUM LEAP" IS MUCH BETTER IN SCI-FI THA

SARAH AND I HAVE BEEN IN ENGLAND VISITING RELATIVES FOR THE PAST THREE WEEKS.

I THINK WE'VE BEEN SENT SO WE CAN RECONNECT WITH THE "HOMELAND."

OR SO THAT SARAH CAN DEVELOP MORE "INDEPENDENCE."

I'M SO SICK OF HER, AND I'M SURE SHE'S SICK OF ME.

MOVE IT, DORK!

SARAH

GOD!!

WE KEEP FIGHTING.

EVEN ON THE PLANE OVER SHE HAD A TOTAL MELTDOWN.

SHE WAS MAD BECAUSE I KICKED HER ASS PLAYING THE CARD GAME SHE THINKS SHE'S SO GOOD AT.

SHE REALLY SCRATCHED ME BADLY THIS TIME...

GRANDMA IS GETTING ON MY NERVES TOO.

MORNING, MICHAEL.

ONCE YOU GET AN IDEA IN HER HEAD YOU CAN'T GET IT BACK OUT.

EVERY TIME I MAKE A JOKE SHE TAKES IT LITERALLY AND CAN'T BE CONVINCED OTHERWISE.

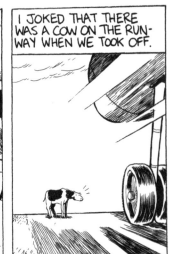

I JOKED THAT THERE WAS A COW ON THE RUNWAY WHEN WE TOOK OFF.

I TOLD HER THE PLANE HAD TO VEER OFF THE RUNWAY TO AVOID HITTING IT.

SCREEEEEEE

SHE STILL THINKS IT'S TRUE AND KEEPS TELLING PEOPLE ABOUT IT.

GRANDMA DOES MAKE ME LAUGH A LOT TOO, THOUGH. SHE TOLD US A STORY ABOUT HOW SHE FARTED IN THE GIRLS' CHOIR WHEN SHE WAS LITTLE.

IT WAS HILARIOUS!

WE'VE ALSO SEEN A LOT OF MY UNCLE JOHN FROM SCOTLAND. HE'S A LOT OF FUN.

I WISH WE SAW EACH OTHER MORE. I FEEL LIKE IF WE DIDN'T LIVE IN OTHER COUNTRIES WE'D BE CLOSE.

I SENT POSTCARDS TO EVERYONE AT HOME.

I WROTE A LETTER TO ROB AND ONE TO WILLIE AS WELL.

I REALIZED THAT I BARELY SAW HER ALL SUMMER LONG. IT'S WEIRD.

SHE DOESN'T HANG OUT WITH US AS MUCH ANYMORE. I GUESS SHE'S GOT A WHOLE OTHER GROUP NOW.

WHAT HAPPENED?

THAT'S ANOTHER THING ABOUT GRANDMA: SHE CAN'T GET WILLIE'S NAME RIGHT.

SHE KEEPS PRONOUNCING IT "WINCEY," EVEN THOUGH I KEEP CORRECTING HER.

SHE CALLS HER "THAT WINCEY" – IT DRIVES ME CRAZY!!

LAST WEEK SARAH AND I WENT BACK TO LEIGHTON BUZZARD ON THE TRAIN.

WE WERE BOTH SURPRISED TO SEE HOW SMALL OUR OLD HOUSE SEEMS TO US NOW.

WE SAW SOME KIDS WE USED TO KNOW FROM THE NEIGHBORHOOD.

WOTCHA MIKE.

THEY TOLD US ABOUT THE NEW OWNERS OF OUR OLD HOUSE.

THEY SAID THE NEW DAD IS ALWAYS WEARING CAMOUFLAGE PANTS.

THEY LAUGHED WHEN I KEPT SAYING "PANTS." TO ENGLISH PEOPLE THAT WORD MEANS UNDERWEAR.

THEY ALSO THOUGHT IT WAS FUNNY WHEN I SAID "BACKYARD" INSTEAD OF "GARDEN":

"YAHHRRD."

HA HA!

YOU SOUND REALLY AMERICAN NOW, MICHAEL.

YOU SHOULD SEE THE GIRLS WE'VE GOT IN AMERICA - THEY'RE REALLY CUTE!

HAHA!

"KYEWWT"

THEY ASKED IF WE SAID WORDS LIKE "FUCK" AND "SHIT" IN AMERICA.

I SAID WE DID; WE TALK LIKE THAT ALL THE TIME.

NOVEMBER 30, 1992

DOINK

GAK!

WAKE UP, MICHAEL, IT'S TIME FOR SCHOOL.

YEAHHH- MANFRED MANN, THOSE GUYS WERE THE BEST, MAN... STICK AROUND AFTER THESE MESSAGES... WE'VE GOT... **LAYLA!**

AND REMEMBER AT TEN TONIGHT WE'RE OPENING THE PHONE LINES... THE 102ND CALLER IS GOING TO WIN TICKETS TO SEE QUEEN GUITARIST BRIAN MAY ON HIS SOLO TOUR NEXT YEAR...

I AM FINALLY READING "ON THE ROAD" BY JACK KEROUAC. I'M ABOUT TWENTY PAGES INTO IT.

IT'S PRETTY GOOD.

I FEEL ONE DAY I WILL TRAVEL ACROSS COUNTRY.

I WANTED TO LEAVE A FEW MONTHS AGO BUT ROB TALKED ME INTO WAITING AND THEN I SIMPLY FORGOT ABOUT IT.

I DON'T THINK I'D BE ABLE TO DO IT ALONE, BECAUSE I AM NOT AS STRONG WHEN I AM BY MYSELF.

I NEED SOMEONE LIKE ROB OR NEIL TO BRING OUT MY CHARACTER SO I CAN BE MYSELF.

THE ONLY PROBLEM WITH "ON THE ROAD" IS THAT HE HAS REALLY ONLY SAID WHAT ROADS HE TOOK AND WHAT INTERSECTIONS MET WHAT.

HE JUST LISTS STUFF LIKE "I TOOK ROUTE 9 AND THEN ROUTE 10". IT'S LIKE READING SOMEONE'S DRIVING DIRECTIONS.

THE CHARACTER (JACK KEROUAC, I PRESUME) HAS JOINED A DRUNK NOW.

RRIIINNG

SO I'M THINKING, MAYBE THE STORY WILL PICK UP.

HEY PETAR, HEY RACHEL.

HEY MIKE.

WHER'RE YOU GOING?

GYM.

OKAY, COOL, SEE YOU AT LUNCH.

SEE YA.

BYE GUYS.

PETAR IS DATING RACHEL NOW.

SHE MOVED HERE A FEW MONTHS AGO FROM VIRGINIA.

I AM MADLY IN LOVE WITH HER.

THERE'S NOTHING I CAN DO ABOUT IT, THOUGH.

I CAN'T HURT PETAR OR STAND IN THE WAY OF HIS AND RACHEL'S LOVE.

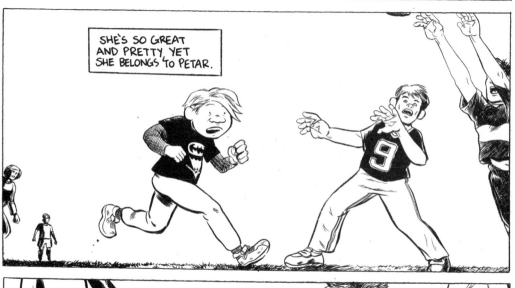

SHE'S SO GREAT AND PRETTY, YET SHE BELONGS TO PETAR.

I HOPE MY DAY WITH HER WILL COME.

RACHEL DID ACTUALLY END UP BEING THE FIRST GIRL I WAS REALLY "IN LOVE" WITH.

MY BROTHER GOT MARRIED IN THE SUMMER OF 1993, AND I INVITED RACHEL TO THE WEDDING AS MY DATE.

WE FIRST KISSED THAT NIGHT, OUT BY A LAKE, OUTSIDE OF THE RECEPTION HALL.

WE DATED FOR ALL OF SENIOR YEAR, AND I REMEMBER I WAS HAPPY THE WHOLE TIME.

I FINALLY HAD A SERIOUS GIRLFRIEND, AS WELL AS A CAR AND AN EASY ACADEMIC YEAR.

I'D SAVED UP ALL OF MY ELECTIVES —

SO WAS ABLE TO TAKE TWO ART CLASSES, DRAMA, CRAFTS, AND CREATIVE WRITING.

THE ONLY TWO CLASS PERIODS RUINING MY OTHERWISE FLAWLESS SCHOOL-DAY CURRICULUM WERE GYM AND "MATH ANALYSIS".

I THINK THE FACT THAT THE REST OF MY DAY WAS SO EASY MADE THAT STUPID MATH CLASS ALL THE WORSE.

I WROTE "RAW" POEMS ABOUT MY FEELINGS AND PUBLISHED THEM IN MY FIRST "FANZINE" ALONG WITH SOME NEW COMICS.

He's a red headed girl,
he's invisible,
he is in the shadows
he is everywhere.

In every crevice of my mind
He fills it and I can't escape.

I've never met Phil.
I don't know him.

Yet I hate him
I would kill him if I could,
If it would do any good,
If it would bring her back,
If there was a point in it.

"This is my boyfriend Phil"
Her boyfriend.
"I love him"
"I'd like you to meet him,
I'd like you to entertain him,
amuse him,
and in the process
kill yourself."   -MD

MY COMICS THIS TIME WERE ABOUT AN ANGRY COLLEGE FRESHMAN WHO DECIDES TO BECOME A SUPERHERO CALLED "THE TARGET."

HIS OUTFIT WAS INSPIRED BY THE COVER TO A GRUNGE-ROCK COMPILATION ALBUM CALLED "NO ALTERNATIVE" I HAD A SHIRT OF.

I WANTED HIM TO BE A REALISTIC, GRITTY CRIME FIGHTER WITH NO SUPERPOWERS, JUST A METAL PIPE HE USED AS A WEAPON.

I ENDED THE FIRST STORY AFTER I HAD HIM GET INTO A FIGHT WITH A MUGGER.

I'M NOT SURE I COULD THINK OF WHAT WOULD REALISTICALLY HAPPEN IF A COLLEGE FRESHMAN REALLY ASSAULTED SOMEONE WITH A PIPE.

EVEN AFTER GETTING OVER RACHEL, I CONTINUED CREATING COMICS.

ALIZA AND I MET IN A BAR.

SHE HATES IT WHEN I TELL PEOPLE THAT.

SHE THINKS IT MAKES THE WHOLE THING SOUND SEEDY OR SOMETHING.

A MUTUAL FRIEND HAD ACTUALLY THROWN A PARTY AT THE BAR.

BUT TECHNICALLY IT'S THE TRUTH.

IT WAS A LAUNCH PARTY FOR A NEW WEB SITE.

IT WAS VALENTINE'S DAY, 2002.

SO THAT'S A NICE TOUCH TO THE WHOLE HOW-WE-MET STORY.

I REMEMBER EXACTLY WHAT SHE WAS WEARING, AND AT LEAST FOUR THINGS THAT WE DISCUSSED.

ONE: WHAT WE DID FOR OUR LIVINGS. PRETTY TYPICAL THING TO COME UP IN CONVERSATION.

I WAS A WEB PRODUCER AT AN INTERNET START-UP AND SHE'D BEEN WORKING IN SALES, BUT WAS GOING TO TRY A CAREER IN INVESTMENT BANKING.

TWO: WHERE WE WERE ON 9/11, ALSO A FAIRLY STANDARD TOPIC IN NEW YORK AT THAT TIME.

I HAD BEEN AT WORK UPTOWN, AND SHE'D BEEN AT HOME IN HER APARTMENT DOWNTOWN.

NEITHER OF US HAD KNOWN ANYONE WHO'D BEEN KILLED.

THREE: COMIC BOOKS. I CAME CLEAN ABOUT BEING A HUGE COMIC BOOK NERD, AND SHE TOLD ME THE NAMES OF THE COMICS THAT SHE'D READ.

A SANDMAN BOOK AND "THE LEAGUE OF EXTRAORDINARY GENTLEMEN" BY ALAN MOORE.

I SUGGESTED THAT SHE TRY READING THE NEW JIMMY CORRIGAN BOOK BY CHRIS WARE.

FOUR: LED ZEPPELIN.

I WAS TRYING (AGAIN) TO GET "INTO" THEM, AND WAS REALLY AMUSED BY ALL OF THE "LORD OF THE RINGS" LYRICS IN SOME OF THEIR SONGS LIKE "RAMBLE ON".

SHE LIVED RIGHT ACROSS THE STREET FROM THE BUILDING USED ON THE COVER OF THE "PHYSICAL GRAFFITI" ALBUM.

I DUNNO, IT KIND OF SOUNDS A BIT LAME WHEN I DESCRIBE IT LIKE THAT - IT'S NOT LIKE WE TALKED ABOUT ALL THESE PROFOUND TOPICS OR ANYTHING.

BUT IT WAS REALLY AN EASY AND FUN CONVERSATION, YOU KNOW? WE JUST STARTED TALKING AND WENT ALL NIGHT.

ACTUALLY, BEFORE ALIZA SHOWED UP, I'D BEEN TALKING TO ANOTHER GIRL WHO WAS SOMEHOW INVOLVED IN FILM.

I'D BROUGHT UP THAT I WAS A CARTOONIST, AND WE ALL OF A SUDDEN GOT INTO THIS HEAVY CONVERSATION ABOUT "HIGH ART."

IT WASN'T EASY AT ALL - I GUESS BECAUSE WE WERE STRANGERS AND MAYBE BOTH FELT LIKE WE DIDN'T WANT TO SOUND DUMB AS WE TALKED ALL "HIGH-BROW."

IT WAS JUST SO DIFFERENT WITH ALIZA.

WE STARTED TALKING ON THAT COUCH, AND I GUESS WE'VE NEVER STOPPED SINCE.

OH YEAH, MY FRIEND ROB, WHOM I KNEW FROM HIGH SCHOOL, WAS ALSO THERE.

WE BOTH GRADUATED MIDDLE-TOWN SOUTH IN 1994.

THEN ME, ROB, AND MY FRIEND NEIL ALL GOT A TRIPLE-OCCUPANCY ROOM AT RUTGERS THE NEXT FALL.

WE LIVED TOGETHER FRESHMAN YEAR, AND THEN AGAIN IN A HOUSE WITH A BUNCH OF GUYS WHEN WE WERE JUNIORS.

I GRADUATED ART SCHOOL IN 1998 AND THEN FLOUNDERED ABOUT FOR A BIT, TRYING TO FIGURE OUT WHAT A DEGREE IN PAINTING COULD BE USED FOR IN THE REAL WORLD.

CARICATURES

LUCKILY IT WAS STILL THE DAYS OF THE DOT-COM BOOM, AND QUALIFICATIONS WEREN'T TOTALLY NECESSARY FOR GETTING OKAY JOBS.

I STARTED WORKING IN NEW YORK, AND ROB ENDED UP FINDING A JOB IN AN OFFICE ONLY A FEW BLOCKS AWAY FROM ME.

OCCASIONALLY WE'D GET LUNCH, BUT MOSTLY WE'D KEEP IN TOUCH BY BICKERING WITH EACH OTHER ON "IM" ALL DAY LONG.

A FEW TIMES I REMEMBER US "HITTING THE TOWN" LOOKING TO SCORE, BUT I DON'T REMEMBER US "GETTING LUCKY" TOO OFTEN.

I WAS PRETTY SURE I WAS GOING TO GO HOME WITH ALIZA THAT NIGHT, THOUGH.

IT WAS GETTING LATE AND PRETTY MUCH EVERYONE ELSE HAD LEFT THE PARTY EXCEPT ME, ALIZA, AND ROB.

I FIGURED ONCE ROB LEFT THEN ME AND ALIZA WOULD HEAD OUT TOGETHER.

BUT HE NEVER GOT THE HINT.

EVENTUALLY, AFTER GETTING HER NUMBER, I HUGGED ALIZA GOODBYE, AND ROB AND I WENT TO THE SUBWAY.

I YELLED AT HIM THE WHOLE WAY ABOUT HIM BEING A POOR "WINGMAN" AND NOT LEAVING ME AND ALIZA ALONE.

TO THIS DAY SHE INSISTS SHE WOULDN'T HAVE GONE HOME WITH ME ANYWAY.

I DON'T BELIEVE HER, AND LIKE TO POINT OUT WE CAN NEVER REALLY KNOW THE TRUTH.

Hard Rock

A FEW MONTHS LATER...

♪ THIS IS WEEKEND EDITION ♪

GOOD MORNING, "CAVEY."

GRUNT

YOU ALWAYS SLEEP IN YOUR PILLOW CAVE.

mm.

DO YOU WANT TO GO IN THE SHOWER FIRST?

I DEFINITELY NEED TO STAY AT MY OWN APARTMENT TONIGHT.

I FEEL LIKE I HAVEN'T DONE ANY DRAWING LATELY...

UM, OKAÁY...

DON'T ACT LIKE IT'S MY FAULT YOU'VE NOT BEEN WORKING.

IT'S NOT...

I JUST FEEL LIKE I HAVEN'T DONE ANYTHING ALL WEEK...

AND NOW WE'RE GOING TO BE IN NEW JERSEY ALL DAY.

WELL, THAT'S NOT MY FAULT EITHER - IT'S YOUR PARENTS WE'RE GOING TO SEE, NOT MINE.

NO, I KNOW...

I'M JUST SAYING -

I DEFINITELY NEED TO GO TO MY PLACE TONIGHT SO I CAN WORK...

SHORTLY

DO YOU THINK YOUR PARENTS WILL SERVE ME HAGGIS AGAIN?

mm

OH, I DUNNO.

THAT SERIOUSLY ISN'T SOMETHING WE'RE ALWAYS EATING AT MY PARENTS'.

IT REALLY WASN'T BAD, I'M TELLING YOU.

THAT'S THE FIRST TIME THEY SERVED IT TO A VISITOR.

OH, I LOVE IT.

DON'T GET ME WRONG.

WHAT TIME IS IT? I DUNNO IF WE'RE GOING TO MAKE OUR TRAIN.

IT'S ALMOST NOON.

SHIT...

SO, ARE YOU FEELING ANY BETTER?

mm?

OH YEAH... I THINK I JUST NEEDED SOME COFFEE.

mm

ONE HOUR AND FORTY MINUTES LATER

HI

HULLO!

SO, YOU KNOW THAT YOUR MUM'S GOING TO BE IN ENGLAND AT THE SAME TIME AS YOU, RIGHT?

VISITING GRANDMA.

YEAH, I KNOW, BUT WE'RE REALLY ONLY GOING TO BE IN LONDON THE ONE NIGHT.

THE POINT OF THE TRIP IS TO GO TO ITALY, NOT ENGLAND.

DON'T YOU THINK YOU'LL HAVE TIME TO NIP UP TO RUGBY AND SEE HER WHILE YOU'RE THERE?

NO, I DEFINITELY DO NOT.

AND DON'T EITHER OF YOU GO TELLING GRANDMA THAT I'M OVER THERE.

I DON'T WANT HER GETTING UPSET THAT I DIDN'T COME TO VISIT.

ALRIGHT THEN, I WON'T TELL HER.

THAT'S A SHAME, THOUGH— IT'S ONLY A TWO-HOUR TRAIN RIDE UP FROM LONDON...

MOM.

SO, IF YOU'RE STOPPING IN ENGLAND ON THE WAY THERE AND BACK— THEN THAT'S FOUR DIFFERENT PLANES YOU'RE GOING ON?

ugh, I WOULDN'T LIKE THAT.

NO, I'M NOT HAPPY ABOUT THAT EITHER...

ARE YOU SCARED OF FLYING, TOO, ALIZA?

ME?

NO.

IT DOESN'T BOTHER ME.

I KNOW MIKE DOESN'T LIKE IT, BUT I DON'T THINK THAT SHOULD STOP US FROM GOING PLACES.

JUST BECAUSE HE'S AFRAID.

I REALLY DIDN'T USE TO HAVE A PROBLEM.

WHEN I WAS A KID IT DIDN'T BOTHER ME.

I REMEMBER THE FIRST TIME I GOT SCARED OF FLYING.

IT WAS WHEN I WENT TO SCOTLAND WITH MY FRIEND NEIL.

IT WAS A SUPER-TURBULENT LANDING IN A RAIN-STORM...

I WAS LITERALLY AFRAID FOR MY LIFE.

IT WAS ONE OF THOSE LANDINGS WHERE EVERYONE CLAPPED WHEN WE FINALLY TOUCHED DOWN.

I'VE JUST HATED IT SINCE.

REMEMBER THAT FLIGHT BACK FROM ENGLAND AFTER GRANDAD DIED?

WHEN IT WAS JUST ME AND YOU?

OH YEAH.

SARAH'S A BAD FLYER TOO.

IT WAS INCREDIBLY BUMPY - SO BAD THAT WE COULDN'T LAND IN NEW YORK RIGHT AWAY - WE HAD TO CIRCLE FOR LIKE FORTY-FIVE MINUTES.

FINALLY WE START COMING DOWN.

!!!! !!!! !!!! !!!!

WE'RE ABOUT TO LAND WHEN SUDDENLY— RRRRRROAARR!

THE PILOT HAD TO TAKE THE PLANE BACK UP, BECAUSE I GUESS IT WASN'T SAFE TO LAND!

OH, IT WAS TERRIBLE, I WAS FEELING SO SICK BY THEN...

AS SOON AS WE WENT BACK UP I HAD TO GRAB THE BAG IN FRONT OF ME AND

GLORF!

OH, IT STUNK! THE WHOLE CABIN REEKED!

HA HA

HA HA

AND WE HAD TO CIRCLE FOR LIKE ANOTHER HALF HOUR!

DO WE HAVE TO TALK ABOUT SARAH THROWING UP RIGHT BEFORE WE HAVE LUNCH?

THE FOOD'S ALMOST READY- MIKE, DO YOU WANT TO SEE IF ANYONE ELSE WANTS SOMETHING TO DRINK?

ALRIGHT.

DO YOU WANT SOMETHING, ALIZA?

I'LL HAVE A LOOK.

OKAY.

PICK OUT SOME MUSIC TO PUT ON AS WELL.

WHAT DO YOU WANT TO HEAR?

BLONDIE?

DIRE STRAITS?

RICK ASTLEY?

THE SOUNDTRACK TO THE MOVIE "WORKING GIRL"?

HEY SARAH, DID YOU HEAR GEORGE MICHAELS GOT A NEW SONG OUT?

YEAH.

I THOUGHT IT WAS PRETTY GOOD.

BUT WHEN'S HE GOING TO COME OUT WITH A NEW ALBUM?

YEAH.

I LOVE THAT "RE-BOOTY" LINE IN "FREEEK"!

HAHA!

HA HA!

HEY ALIZA,

LOOK AT THIS.

MY PARENTS STILL HAVE THIS...

Queen
A Night At The Opera

Queen
A Night At The Opera

IT'S THE FIRST ALBUM I EVER OWNED.

I'M GOING TO TAKE THIS.

WHEN I WAS A KID MY FAVORITE SONGS ON THIS WERE MOSTLY THE "DEEP CUTS"...

"DEATH ON TWO LEGS"...

"THE PROPHET'S SONG"...

"SEASIDE RENDEZVOUS"...

IT'S INTERESTING, AT THE TIME I HAD NO IDEA THAT ONLY SOME SONGS FROM AN ALBUM GOT ANY RADIO PLAY.

SEE - THAT'S WHAT'S SO SUCKY ABOUT CLASSIC ROCK RADIO STATIONS.

AS MUCH AS I LIKE CLASSIC ROCK - MOST OF THE STATIONS JUST PLAY ALL OF THE SAME SONGS OVER AND OVER.

mm

THEY MAKE IT SEEM LIKE THE ONLY SONGS ON THE RADIO IN THE SEVENTIES WERE "LAYLA" AND THAT MONEY SONG BY PINK FLOYD.

ALRIGHT, ANDREW'S NOT HERE YET, SO WE'RE GOING TO START WITHOUT HIM.

WHO WANTS HOT DOGS?

I'LL HAVE ONE.

THEY PROBABLY ONLY PROGRAM THE STATIONS LIKE THAT SO MORE LISTENERS HAVE A CHANCE OF BEING ABLE TO SING ALONG.

I BET THAT'S WHY THEY DO IT.

I KNEW THIS WOULD HAPPEN...

I'M NOT GOING TO GET TO DO ANY DRAWING TONIGHT.

OH, AM I ABOUT TO GET YELLED AT AGAIN?

NO.

IT'S JUST, TOMORROW I HAVE TO GO TO MY PLACE TO WORK, OK?

OKAY!

IT'S JUST, YOU KNOW, I GET ANXIOUS WHEN I DON'T DRAW FOR A LONG TIME.

I KNOW.

YOU MAKE THAT FACE.

WHAT?

I DO NOT!

WHAT FACE?

YOU FURROW YOUR BROW AND STICK YOUR CHIN ALL OUT.

LIKE THIS.

SHUT UP!

I DO NOT!

DON'T YOU WANT TO WAIT UNTIL WE GET ON THE PLANE?

NO, IT TAKES A WHILE TO KICK IN...

OKAY, JUST LET ME HAVE A HALF.

AND SO...

ZZZZ

LONDON, ENGLAND

HIIYA!

HEL-LO MARV-ELOUS!

MARV, THIS IS MIKE.

HIYA, MIKE.

HI MARV, NICE TO MEET YOU.

COME IN, COME IN - HOW WAS YOUR FLIGHT?

Ugh!

I HATE FLYING!

NAOMI WILL BE HOME SOON.

SO, ARE YOU FROM LONDON, MARV?

I'M FROM ENGLAND MYSELF, YOU KNOW...

LONDON BRIDGE

UGH, I FEEL AWFUL!

COME ON - STAY AWAKE! IT'LL HELP YOU GET OVER YOUR JET LAG QUICKER.

YOU THINK WE'LL GET LUNCH AT THE MUSEUM, NAOMI?

SURE.

WE WILL ROCK YOU

DON'T YOU GUYS WANT TO GO AND SEE THIS?

WHAT'S THAT?

OH, IT'S THAT QUEEN MUSICAL.

NO THANKS!

I THINK WE'LL PASS...

AWW, BUT IT'S ONLY PLAYING IN *LONDON*...

THE NEXT DAY

THANKS AGAIN FOR HAVING US.

OH, NO PROBLEM, SWEETIE.

LOVELY TO MEET YOU, MIKE.

SEE YOU IN TEN DAYS ON THE WAY BACK.

ROME, ITALY

WHY DON'T YOU MIND YOUR OWN BUSINESS?

YOU AR RUDE

OH

IT'S THOSE ITALIANS FIGHTING WITH SOME FRENCH PASSENGER.

JEEZ.

JESUS - WHO THE FUCK STARTS YELLING ON A PLANE THESE DAYS?

I KNOW - THAT SCARED THE SHIT OUT OF ME...

WHAT'S THE MATTER WITH THOSE PEOPLE?

NEW YORK CITY

OH, IT'S SO NICE BEING BACK IN MY OWN BED...

I HAVE A VOICEMAIL.

IT'S FROM MY DAD, LET ME CALL HIM BACK.

HEY DAD.

OH, HI THERE, MIKE.

HOW WAS YOUR TRIP?

IT WAS GREAT!

WHAT'S GOING ON WITH YOU?

WELL, uh, WE'VE HAD SOME, uh, BAD NEWS

OH?

YOUR, uh, GRANDMA HAS, uh, PASSED AWAY THIS MORNING, SO, um...

WHAT?

...YEAH, MY DAD'S GOING OVER RIGHT AWAY TO HELP MY MOM.

I'M GOING TO HAVE TO FIGURE OUT A WAY TO GET OVER TOO, I THINK.

MY DAD TOLD ME THE AIRLINES DO.

SOME SORT OF BEREAVEMENT FLIGHT THING.

YOU CAN GET A CHEAPER FLIGHT.

APPARENTLY YOU HAVE TO PROVIDE THEM WITH A DEATH CERTIFICATE, THOUGH.

WHICH IS A REALLY MORBID THING.

OKAY, I'LL TALK TO YOU LATER...

LOVE YOU TOO.

AND SO

LADIES AND GENTLEMEN, PLEASE TAKE YOUR SEATS

LADIES AND GENTLEME IF YOU WOULD TURN ATTENTION TO THE F WE'D LIKE REVIEW S SAFETY FEATURES BOARD THIS B

I REALLY THINK THEY SHOULDN'T DO THIS SAFETY PROCEDURES THING.

IT JUST REMINDS US ALL THAT THE PLANE MIGHT CRASH.

WE ALL KNOW THAT IF THE PLANE DID CRASH, NONE OF US WOULD SURVIVE BECAUSE OF FOLLOWING THE SAFETY PROCEDURES.

NOBODY EVER SURVIVES A PLANE CRASH - IT'S ALWAYS 100% OF THE PEOPLE ON BOARD ARE KILLED.

HOW DID I GET HERE AGAIN?

FLIGHT ATTENDANTS PLEASE TA YOUR SE

I'M SO SCARED OF DYING.

BRITISH AIRWAYS

BUT THANKFULLY:

HI.

HI MIKE — I'M A FRIEND OF YOUR MUM'S.

TAXI

I'M VERY SORRY ABOUT YOUR GRAN.

OH THANK YOU.

YES, WE WERE ALL WATCHING ON THE TV— SUCH A SHAME WHEN THOSE TOWERS FELL.

YEAH, IT WAS A REALLY AWFUL DAY.

HERE WE ARE.

HI MUM.

ALRIGHT THEN.

THANKS FOR COMING, JOHN.

MICHAEL, DAD'S LEAVING NOW.

GOOAL!!

ALRIGHT, BYE DAD—SEE YOU BACK IN AMERICA.

BYE THEN.

TAKE CARE OF YOUR MUM, OKAY?

I WILL.

AND SO

YOU KNOW, I ASKED ALIZA TO COME WITH ME TO ENGLAND FOR ALL THIS.

OH, I DON'T THINK THAT WOULD HAVE BEEN SUCH A GREAT IDEA ... THIS WOULD HAVE BEEN A BAD TIME.

SHE SEEMS LIKE A NICE GIRL ... YOU SHOULD LET US GET TO KNOW HER IN BETTER CIRCUMSTANCES THAN THIS...

mm

IT'S STRANGE TO THINK...

I WONDER IF I'LL EVER BE BACK TO RUGBY AGAIN.

I DON'T KNOW THAT I'LL BE BACK FOR A LONG TIME.

"WE WILL ROCK YOU" IS A MUSICAL BASED ON THE SONGS OF QUEEN. IT'S SET IN A FAR-OFF DYSTOPIAN FUTURE WHERE THE CULTURE IS HOMOGENOUS AND THERE IS NO ROCK MUSIC.

GALILEO AND SCARAMOUCHE ARE TWO YOUNG DREAMERS WHO YEARN FOR SOMETHING MORE VIBRANT THAN THE BLAND WORLD THAT THEY KNOW.

THE TWO OF THEM TEAM UP WITH A BAND OF OUTLAWS CALLED "THE BOHEMIANS".

THEY QUEST FOR A LOST GUITAR THAT WILL BRING ROCK BACK TO THE WORLD.

IT'S A LITTLE BIT LIKE THE PLOT TO RUSH'S CONCEPT ALBUM "2112".

IT'S ACTUALLY A PRETTY FUNNY SHOW, BUT OF COURSE THE THING I LIKED BEST ABOUT IT WAS THE MUSIC.

I ALWAYS REMEMBER MY FRIEND ORION REMARKING THAT QUEEN HAD SONGS FOR ALL OCCASIONS - WHICH IS WHY I THINK IT WORKED WELL TO WRITE A PLAY STRUCTURED AROUND THEM.

I THINK I REMEMBER HIM SAYING THAT SO WELL BECAUSE I TOOK THE COMPLIMENT PERSONALLY.

I DOUBT ORION HAS A MEMORY OF MAKING THAT REMARK.

I GUESS I'VE ALWAYS FELT SOME SENSE OF OWNERSHIP WHEN IT COMES TO QUEEN MUSIC.

A COMPLIMENT FOR QUEEN IS THE SAME AS AN ENDORSEMENT OF ME.

THE ILLUSION IS RUINED WHEN YOU ENCOUNTER OTHER PEOPLE WHO THINK THEY'RE "SUPER-FANS" TOO.

IT'S BETTER WHEN IT JUST FEELS LIKE IT'S MY THING...

MY GRANDMA ACTUALLY HAD A FAVORITE QUEEN SONG OF HER OWN.

"WHO WANTS TO LIVE FOREVER", FROM "A KIND OF MAGIC," WHICH IS ALSO THE SOUNDTRACK ALBUM TO THE MOVIE "HIGHLANDER" WITH CHRISTOPHER LAMBERT.

HE DUELS FREDDIE MERCURY IN A SWORDFIGHT IN THE MUSIC VIDEO FOR THE THEME SONG "PRINCES OF THE UNIVERSE."

FREDDIE USES HIS FAMOUS CUT-OFF MICROPHONE STAND AS A SWORD.

"WHO WANTS TO LIVE FOREVER" MADE GRANDMA CRY - SHE ASSOCIATED IT WITH AN ENGLISH GIRL WHO DIED OF SOME KIND OF TERMINAL ILLNESS.

I'M NOT SURE WHAT THE CONNECTION WAS, BUT GRANDMA ALWAYS SAID THE SONG MADE HER SAD BECAUSE OF IT.

I DEFINITELY THOUGHT ABOUT MY GRANDMA DURING THAT SONG IN THE SHOW.

WHEN ALIZA AND I GOT MARRIED WE CHOSE "SHE MAKES ME" FROM THE "SHEER HEART ATTACK" ALBUM TO PLAY DURING THE PROCESSIONAL.

IT PLAYED DURING THE PART WHERE I WALKED DOWN THE AISLE WITH MY PARENTS.

WHEN ALIZA CAME DOWN THE AISLE WITH HER PARENTS, WE PLAYED "TILL THERE WAS YOU" FROM "THE MUSIC MAN".

THAT SONG HAS SPECIAL MEANING TO ALIZA AND HER FAMILY.

OF COURSE, I TRIED TO INCORPORATE A FEW QUEEN SONGS INTO THE DANCE MIX FOR THE WEDDING RECEPTION.

UNFORTUNATELY, I'VE ALWAYS FOUND THAT WHILE QUEEN SONGS ROCK, THERE AREN'T A LOT THAT ARE GOOD TO DANCE TO.

I WENT TO A PARTY IN HIGH SCHOOL FOR A GIRL I DIDN'T KNOW ALL THAT WELL.

I'D GOT IT IN MY HEAD THAT A SONG EVERYONE WOULD ENJOY WAS "STONE COLD CRAZY" FROM "SHEER HEART ATTACK".

I THOUGHT IT WOULD BE GOOD TO DANCE TO (THOUGH IT'S NOT REALLY).

I GAVE MY CASSETTE TO THE DJ - I HAD IT ALL CUED UP AND GOOD TO GO.

WHEN HE PUT ON MY TAPE, THOUGH, INSTEAD OF MY SONG, "IN THE LAP OF THE GODS" BLARED OUT OF THE SPEAKERS.

IT TURNED OUT HE'D REWOUND THE TAPE TO THE BEGINNING OF SIDE TWO.

IF YOU'RE FAMILIAR WITH THE ALBUM YOU'D KNOW THAT SONG IS PRETTY OUT THERE, ALL STRANGELY DISTORTED - DEFINITELY NOT GOOD DANCE MUSIC.

NOBODY KNEW WHAT THE HELL IT WAS - I RAN TO MAKE THE DJ TURN IT OFF!

BUT THE WORST WAS THAT I CUED IT UP AGAIN FOR HIM TO PLAY A LITTLE LATER, AND THE EXACT SAME THING HAPPENED!

AND TO TOP IT ALL OFF, I NOW REALIZE THAT NOBODY WOULD HAVE WANTED TO HEAR "STONE COLD CRAZY" IN THE FIRST PLACE!

IF YOU AREN'T FAMILIAR WITH THE SONG I'M TALKING ABOUT, YOU MIGHT NOT REALIZE WHAT A BAD DANCE CHOICE IT IS.

THAT MEMORY STILL MAKES ME CRINGE...

THIS IS WHAT I SEE WHEN I PICTURE THAT NIGHT IN MY HEAD: I'M IN THE CROWD, LOOKING OVER AT THE DJ.

I'M NOT SURE IF THIS IS FROM BEFORE OR AFTER THE INCIDENT WITH MY TAPE

THIS IS THE PICTURE I SEE WHEN I REMEMBER WATCHING GEORGE MICHAEL SING AT THE FREDDIE MERCURY TRIBUTE.

THIS IS WHAT I SEE WHEN I REMEMBER IMAGINING MYSELF SINGING "SOMEBODY TO LOVE" IN THE SCHOOL CAFETERIA.

STRANGE TO HAVE A PICTURE FOR AN INCIDENT THAT NEVER TOOK PLACE ANYWHERE EXCEPT IN MY OWN MIND.

THIS IS THE MEMORY OF THE TIME I IMAGINED MEETING THE MEMBERS OF QUEEN WHEN I WAS TEN YEARS OLD.

I WONDER IF SARAH HAS A MEMORY OF BEING A LITTLE GIRL AND HAVING AN IMAGINARY MEETING WITH GEORGE MICHAEL LIKE MY ONE WITH QUEEN.

WE MUST ALL HAVE MEMORIES OF THE THINGS WE ONCE IMAGINED COMING TRUE.

THINGS THAT WERE ONCE OUR DREAMS, BUT HAVE NOW BECOME ONLY DREAMS WE REMEMBER ONCE HAVING.

I THINK WE ALL FELT A LITTLE BIT OF FAMILY PRIDE AROUND GEORGE MICHAEL'S PERFORMANCE AT THE TRIBUTE CONCERT.

OUT OF EVERYBODY WHO SANG WITH QUEEN, HE WAS CLEARLY THE STANDOUT.

TWO ICONS OF OUR FAMILY MYTHOLOGY.

MY FAVORITE BAND OF ALL TIME PAIRED WITH SARAH'S FAVORITE POP STAR.

IT'S THAT OWNERSHIP AGAIN, BUT IN THIS INSTANCE WE COULD ALL SHARE IN IT.

GEORGE MICHAEL AND QUEEN RELEASED AN ALBUM OF THAT PERFORMANCE CALLED "FIVE LIVE," WHICH WAS ONE OF THE FIRST COMPACT DISCS I EVER OWNED.

I'VE BOUGHT AND ENJOYED EVERY GEORGE MICHAEL CD SINCE - MY FAVORITE BY FAR IS "PATIENCE," RELEASED IN 2004.

SARAH AND I SAW HIM PERFORM ONCE IN 2000 AT A GAY PRIDE FESTIVAL.

SARAH, WHO IS NORMALLY QUIET AND RESERVED, COULDN'T STOP HERSELF FROM SCREAMING LIKE A TEENAGER.

I FINALLY GOT TO SEE QUEEN LIVE, IN A WAY, IN THE FALL OF 2005.

THEY KICKED OFF THE SHOW WITH "TIE YOUR MOTHER DOWN".

BRIAN MAY AND ROGER TAYLOR WENT ON TOUR WITH PAUL RODGERS, THE GUY WHO SANG THAT SONG "ALL RIGHT NOW."

IT WAS THRILLING TO HEAR THAT VERY DISTINCTIVE BRIAN MAY GUITAR LIVE FOR THE FIRST TIME.

THE SHOW WAS FUN, BUT I COULDN'T HELP BUT FEEL SAD THAT I WASN'T SEEING QUEEN WITH FREDDIE MERCURY.

DURING "BOHEMIAN RHAPSODY" THEY PROJECTED FOOTAGE OF HIM SINGING THE SONG ONTO A GIANT SCREEN.

THE CROWD WENT WILD.

CLEARLY THEY ALL LOVED HIM.

I ONCE READ AN INTERVIEW WITH A WRITER WHO SUGGESTED THAT THE URGE TO WRITE AUTOBIOGRAPHY CAME OUT OF A FEAR OF ONE'S OWN MORTALITY.

WHEN I THINK OF QUEEN I CAN REMEMBER MY WHOLE LIFE.

I REMEMBER THE FIRST TIME I EVER HEARD A QUEEN SONG.

I THINK ABOUT "BOHEMIAN RHAPSODY" AND IT REMINDS ME OF AN EVENING WITH GRANDMA AND GRANDAD.

I THINK ABOUT THAT SONG AND IT MAKES ME THINK OF HIGH SCHOOL WHEN FREDDIE MERCURY DIED.

NOW I REMEMBER MOM AND ME GOING TO SEE THE QUEEN MUSICAL AFTER GRANDMA'S FUNERAL.

NOW THE MUSIC MAKES ME THINK OF THAT.

A TRIUMPH!
THE GLOBE

THINGS ARE ALWAYS CHANGING.

BUT THE SONGS STILL SOUND THE SAME NOW AS THEY DID WHEN I WAS YOUNG.

I PRESS PLAY AND THE SAME MUSIC IN THE SAME SEQUENCE COMES OUT EVERY TIME.

BUT THE THOUGHTS THAT ARISE IN MY MIND ARE WHAT START TO DIFFER.

I REMEMBER SPECIFIC MOMENTS.

I THINK OF PEOPLE THAT I CARE ABOUT.

I REMEMBER SO MANY THINGS THAT HAVE HAPPENED IN MY LIFE.

OLD IMPRESSIONS OF MY IMAGINATION SPRING BACK INTO MY MIND'S EYE.

SNAP!

ARE YOU NERVOUS ABOUT MEETING HIM, THEN?

YES! HAHA!

I CAN'T BELIEVE WE JUST SAW HIM SITTING RIGHT OVER THERE...

LOW PRICE!
$7.99

I REALLY DIDN'T THINK THERE'D BE SO MANY PEOPLE.

I KNOW!

THIS LINE IS LONG!

EXIT

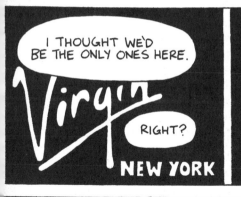

I THOUGHT WE'D BE THE ONLY ONES HERE.

RIGHT?

Virgin

NEW YORK

WE'RE BARELY EVEN MOVING...

PATIENCE

MONDAY, JUNE 14, 2004

HAHA!

ROCK-POP

I CAN'T BELIEVE YOU'RE GOING TO WEAR THAT SHIRT, SARAH.

DON'T MAKE FUN OR I'LL CHANGE MY MIND...

YORK

CHOOSE LIFE

... ANY WAY THE WIND BLOWS ...

MIKE AND SARAH DAWSON, NEW YORK CITY, CIRCA, 1987

Acknowledgments

This book couldn't have been written without the continued love and support of my wife, Aliza. She is an inspiration, and always makes me believe that great things are possible.

Thank you to my family for a lifetime of nothing but encouragement.

Thanks to my pal Alex Robinson for many Wednesday nights at Foley's talking about the rewarding world of comics and life in general. To PJ Mark for taking on this book and finding some amazing homes for it, and Yelena Gitlin, Dan Franklin, and Colin Dickerman for helping me to shape this story into its final form.

I am especially grateful to the following friends and family: Chris Radtke, Gary Gretsky, Robert Poole, Kristen Siebecker, Vania Tseng, Tony Consiglio, Jonathan Bennett, Luke Harms, Brandi Kattan, Nancy Tsai, John Kerschbaum, and the Best family: Marc, Betsy, Micah, and Jen.

Very special thanks to Chris Pitzer of AdHouse Books.

Thanks also to James Boyle, Charles Brownstein, Jeff Cioletti, Alain David, Vito Delsante, Christian Dumais, Serge Ewenczyk, Aaron F. Gonzalez, Dean Haspiel, Brian Jacks, Phil Jackson, Damien Jay, Tom Kaczynski, Charlie LaGreca, Heidi MacDonald, Jeff Manley, Janna Morishima, Alex Ness, Mark Nevins, Mike O'Connor, Annette Rella, Stephen Schwartz, Casey Seijas, Dave Sim, Chris Staros, Alexandria Steppe, Cynthia Stierle, Adam Suerte, Jennifer and Francis Tunney, Brett Warnock, Mike Watanabe, Rich Watson, and Caleb Wright.

And, of course, thanks to Freddie, Brian, Roger, and John.

Lyric Credits

"Bicycle Race": Words and music by Freddie Mercury © 1978 Queen Music Ltd. All rights for the U.S and Canada controlled and administered by Beechwood Music Corp. All rights for the world excluding the U.S. and Canada controlled and administered by EMI Music Publishing Ltd. All rights reserved. International copyright secured. Used by permission. "Bohemian Rhapsody": Words and music by Freddie Mercury © 1975 (renewed 2003) Queen Music Ltd. All rights for the U.S and Canada controlled and administered by Glenwood Music Corp. All rights for the world excluding the U.S. and Canada controlled and administered by EMI Music Publishing Ltd. All rights reserved. International copyright secured. Used by permission. "Death on Two Legs (Dedicated to...)": Words and music by Freddie Mercury © 1975 (renewed 2003) Queen Music Ltd. All rights for the U.S and Canada controlled and administered by Glenwood Music Corp. All rights for the world excluding the U.S. and Canada controlled and administered by EMI Music Publishing Ltd. All rights reserved. International copyright secured. Used by permission. "Don't Stop Me Now": Words and music by Freddie Mercury © 1978 Queen Music Ltd. All rights for the U.S and Canada controlled and administered by Beechwood Music Corp. All rights for the world excluding the U.S. and Canada controlled and administered by EMI Music Publishing Ltd. All rights reserved. International copyright secured. Used by permission. "The Fairy Feller's Master-Stroke": Words and music by Freddie Mercury © 1974 (renewed 2002) Queen Music Ltd. All rights for the U.S and Canada controlled and administered by Beechwood Music Corp. All rights for the world excluding the U.S. and Canada controlled and administered by EMI Music Publishing Ltd. All rights reserved. International copyright secured. Used by permission. "I Want to Break Free": Words and music by John Deacon © 1984 Queen Music Ltd. All rights for the U.S and Canada controlled and administered by Beechwood Music Corp. All rights for the world excluding the U.S. and Canada controlled and administered by EMI Music Publishing Ltd. All rights reserved. International copyright secured. Used by permission. "The Show Must Go On": Words and music by Freddie Mercury, Brian May, Roger Taylor, and John Deacon © 1991 Queen Music Ltd. All rights for the U.S and Canada controlled and administered by Beechwood Music Corp. All rights for the world excluding the U.S. and Canada controlled and administered by EMI Music Publishing Ltd. All rights reserved. International copyright secured. Used by permission. "Somebody to Love": Words and music by Freddie Mercury, Brian May, Roger Taylor, and John Deacon © 1976 (renewed 2004) Queen Music Ltd. All rights for the U.S and Canada controlled and administered by Beechwood Music Corp. All rights for the world excluding the U.S. and Canada controlled and administered by EMI Music Publishing Ltd. All rights reserved. International copyright secured. Used by permission. "Uptown Girl": Words and music by Billy Joel © 1983 Joelsongs. All rights reserved. International copyright secured. Used by permission.